Textbook 1

1

GW01454379

课本（上册）

Zoom In: Elementary Chinese in 60 Hours

60 小时突破初级中文

主　编：LIQUN SU（苏立群）
副主编：WEI-SAN SU（胡未三）
编写者：LIQUN SU（苏立群）
　　　　WEI-SAN SU（胡未三）
　　　　王 岩

MP3
www.sinolingua.com.cn

Sinolingua
华语教学出版社

First Edition   2021

ISBN 978-7-5138-2063-9
Copyright 2021 by Sinolingua Co., Ltd
Published by Sinolingua Co., Ltd
24 Baiwanzhuang Street, Beijing 100037, China
Tel: (86) 10-68320585   68997826
Fax: (86) 10-68997826   68326333
http://www.sinolingua.com.cn
E-mail: hyjx@sinolingua.com.cn
Facebook: www.facebook.com/sinolingua
Printed by Beijing Hucais Culture Communication Co., Ltd

Printed in the People's Republic of China

During my twenty years of teaching at SOAS (School of Oriental and African Studies, University of London), I began to develop an interest in different ways of teaching Chinese as a written language. My book *Mastering Chinese Characters: A Modern Approach* was published in 2014 by the Commercial Press. I've now compiled a new series of textbooks which is an update called the *Zoom In* series (including *Elementary Chinese in 60 Hours* 1 & 2, *Intermediate Chinese in 118 Hours* 1 & 2, *Advanced Chinese in 337 Hours* 1 & 2 with accompanying workbooks).

The traditional way to teach written Chinese has been to take each character apart and trace the roots of its radicals to their sources. Though being well-accepted by Chinese students who are already familiar with their own history and culture, this approach has not been particularly effective for foreign students learning the language from scratch. In hindsight, this strategy was perhaps both too academic and too localised. It tended to assume the student possessed a basic knowledge of China such as its national and folkloric heritage, its geography, social values and codes of behaviour.

In an attempt to avoid similar pitfalls, it became something of an obsession of mine to figure out an alternative way to inspire and support foreign students in a way which does not require prior knowledge of Chinese. The resulting series of textbooks is an attempt at this more intuitive approach, that employs fresh visual tools. Since both pictures and sound are regular components of Chinese characters, we have included a cartoon to match each character, supported by a short piece of text in English which students are encouraged to read aloud. Whatever proved most helpful to the class or individual ended up on these pages, as I believe the priority should always be given to practical use over established convention.

In accordance with the Chinese saying, "Give a man a fish and you feed him for a day; teach a man to fish and you feed him for a lifetime. Knowledge is the best charity," the book encourages students to follow the method and pursue their own learning goals as far as their interest dictates.

The first 15 lessons are dedicated to character learning while the later lessons include two parts. "Part 1 Combining Characters" is about making words or phrases. All 178 characters learned in the first 15 lessons are used to form words and phrases. "Part II Compose Sentences" is about using words and phrases to form five sentences. The first three sentences are simple and the last two are longer and more difficult. After finishing the whole book, students should be able to know 1,000 words or phrases and read 534 simple sentences, while those with strong language ability could master as many as 890 sentences.

A workbook is also designed to help students memorize Chinese characters and word combinations as well as helping to construct sentences with those words. The book also provides a story of some 3,000 words for students to read.

This series has been used in the classroom for two years. One of the courses was held from Sept 14, 2017 to Nov 24, 2017. 14 students spent 1.5 hours per week in a total of ten weeks (15 hours) to learn 178 Chinese characters. They spent another 15 hours to learn words, phrases, and sentences to finish the whole book, which helped them pass easily the test for lower beginner level of Chinese language.

In the West there exists tremendous interest in learning Chinese. In order to follow this trend, I would suggest a couple of things: Firstly, to remind Chinese language teachers that a spoken language and its written form are intimately connected. In other words, to teach the spoken language, it is paramount to teach reading and writing at the same time. Secondly, our attention should be given more to children and teenagers, for whom Chinese has become one of the most popular subjects at school. It is with this age group in mind that we hope to take on a serious subject in a relaxed and playful manner.

As this volume is soon to be put into publication, I would like to take the opportunity to thank Dr. Zhou Shoujin, Emily Ingram, Dr. Peter Levell, Simona Bryant, Carolyn Choa, Maha H Ibrahim and everyone else who has made generous contributions. Special thanks go to Mr. Kevin Munns for his recording of the English in the book. His high standard of English has greatly helped improve the book!

David Su Liqun

前言 Preface

任教英国伦敦大学亚非学院（School of Oriental and African Studies, University of London）的 20 年期间，我一直都在寻找一种向欧美学生介绍汉字的方法。"突破中文"系列教材是在《汉字图解学习手册》（Mastering Chinese Characters: A Modern Approach，商务印书馆 2014）的基础上运用更新思路编写的。该系列教材共分六个级别：《60 小时突破初级中文（上、下册）》、《118 小时突破中级中文（上、下册）》和《337 小时突破高级中文（上、下册）》，每个级别含课本和练习册各一册。

《60 小时突破初级中文（上册）》课本的第一部分（字篇，第一课到第十五课）学习汉字。

在对外汉语教学的数十年中，曾不断有人尝试过以"图片解析汉字"的方法来编写教材，不过总体来说收效不明显，原因是这些书对汉字的解释过于"学术化"与"地域化"。"学术化"是指"以文解文，以字解字"，忽略了学习者是外国人，他们对中国是"零知识"；"地域化"是指著书者大多对欧美受众群体的社会及价值观缺乏切身的了解，因而，在文化的沟通和语言的表达两个方面都受到了局限。这套"突破中文"系列教材尽量避免这些短处，而采用的方法是：第一，把学生领回到甲骨文、金文和籀文时代——对这个久远的时光隧道本书不是用"引证"和"六书"去充填，而是通过卡通画的形象并结合汉字后面的故事把这些字"激活"来启发、引导学生；第二，采用了以"声"加深学生对"形"记忆的特殊模式，即每一个汉字都设计了"把汉字说出来"的一条，就是用一句地道的英文把这个汉字的形、声、义都归纳、融合进去，达到"只要记得住这句话，就知道这个字的意思、写法和发音"的目的。此外，课本还提供了书写的笔顺，鼓励学习者"唱字"，"横竖撇捺，点勾折提"边写边唱。

课本的第二部分（词句篇，第十六课到第三十课）是学习汉字的组构功能，即以字组词、以词组句、以句组段、以段组章的规律。

解释这个规律之前，需要先把这套书何以取名"Zoom In（趋真向实法则）"或称"Natural Flow（自然顺序法，简称'序法'）"做一个说明。

什么是这个"趋真向实法则"（或"自然顺序法"）呢？众所周知，大自然里有两个相互独立又相互制约的元素，一个是时间，一个是空间。宇宙中的万物在穿过时间隧道时都在改变其空间的位置；所以这个"自然顺序法"是时间先于空间，而时间自身的顺序是由无限的长到有限的短，空间自身的顺序是由无限的大到有限的小。人类的生活也不例外，这两个元素的规则影响着我们的万千世界。耐人寻味的是这个"自然顺序法"从数千年以前就反射到中华民族的语言（汉语）中，汉语的"序法"规则就是建立在这个基础之上的。

具体来说，两个或两个以上的汉字首尾相接的法则，在表达时间时是"由长到短"，表达空间时是由"大到小"。更具体来说，这个"序法（自然顺序法）"反映到汉语的字词与句子的组构方面，都是从广义到狭义，从整体到局部，从一般到具体，从前到后，从上到下，等等。

中国古代的智者说："给人一条鱼，你只喂他一天；教给一个人会钓鱼，你就养活了他一辈子；授人以技能是最好的助人方式。"基于汉语这种简单易懂的"序法"，课本的第二部分（第十六课到第三十课）就是把这个"序法"用在"以字组词，以词组句"上——教授学习者钓鱼的技能！

于此，课本里后十五课的内容都是使用第一部分学习的 178 个初级汉字去组构词、短语的，而且，每个汉字都给出五个使用该汉字的句子，其中前三句比较简单，后两句相对长些、复杂些。在本书的最后一课结束的时候，学生能够认读 1000 个单词或短语，可以掌握 534 个简单句子；对于那些语言能力强的人，可以达到 890 个句子。此外，每本还配有练习册，提供记忆汉字和字词扩充及中英句子互翻的练习。为了增加学生的成就感，本书还附有一篇长达 3000 个汉字的小说供学生阅读欣赏。

《60 小时突破初级中文（上册）》（含课本及练习册）从完成初稿到最终提交用了两年多的时间，其间，它已被作为课堂教材试用过多次。粗粗统计的结果是，如果学生每周上课或自学 1.5 小时，经过 20 周共 30 个小时的学习，通过初等低阶水平的考试是绰绰有余的。

苏立群

用序法学习中文，快速又容易

序法，是我在英国 30 多年执教汉语总结出来的一种教非母语的汉语学习者学习汉语的简易、快捷方法。

几十年前我在大学就读的是话剧舞台表演和语言专业。这个特殊的专业成为 20 世纪 80 年代伦敦大学亚非学院接纳我做汉语老师的主要原因。不过，直到我面对英国和欧洲的学生的时候才发现，手头所有的汉语语法理论和教材都是用印欧语系的理念编写的，而我自己的母语则"没有语法"，连我在中国学到的"主谓宾定状补"都是源于这个外来的体系。

后来，真正站到讲台上，我渐渐地发现，在这个洋语系解构下的中文留下了不少"空白点"（以英语为例，没有对等的字、词及结构做参照）。为了解决这个问题，诸多有汉语专业的大学（包括英国伦敦大学亚非学院）把这些语法的难点设置为"博士学位"，期待来自中国的学者诠释这些疑难。在这种情况下，我一多半出于好奇、一少半出于教学所需，决心返朴归真，回到古代，从汉语的"自性"中去寻找法则。

经过长达二十年的大学执教，我的思路逐渐成熟了，于是在 2007 初我便辞去了教职，投入了对汉语"自性"规律的研究，同时，建立了一个自己的语言机构——"英国子午文院"。

概言之，西方语言学的一些基本理念与汉语的实际情况可以用"大相径庭"四个字来描述。如，"一切语言都是创造语音在前，形成文字在后""古老的汉字终将消亡在数码时代而由拼音来替代"诸论。其实，中国语言文字的形成与印欧语系有很大的差别。究其源，与早期中国文明中最重要的"占卜在先，行事在后"有直接关系。"卜辞"是记述占卜时间、内容、过程和检验结果的文本（前辞—命辞—卜辞—验辞），卜文的孰先孰后客观地反映着古人行事的顺序，即，在某时（天）——于某地（地）——何种活动（为）及结果；在这三段式的末段，即"何为"，是句子的"核心目的词"（以下用简称"核目词"）。这个固定的格式虽然是卦辞所诉，实际上，它决定着古人从事各种社会活动的先后顺序。这个起源于占卜、实践于古人生活的纪实方式，日后衍化成了汉语的"序法"。汉语是一种"我口说我做，我手记我行"的语言体系。即：文字如实记录行为的顺序，就是正确的汉语。

具体来说，汉语中一个标准的、包含时空的陈述句，是按照天（时间）—地（地点）—为（行为）的顺序排列的。一个句子无论字数多少，都是这种直白的纪录方式。比如一句话有 5 个汉字，若是每个汉字用一个阿拉伯序数的整数来表示，分别是①－②－③－④－⑤，数学知识告诉我们，②要紧随着①，③要紧随着②，④要紧随着③等……如果是 6 个汉字，就是①－②－③－④－⑤－⑥，而不能是②－①－④－③－⑥－⑤；如果是十个汉字就是①－②－③－④－⑤－⑥－⑦－⑧－⑨－⑩，不可以是别的顺序，也就是说，不可以任意调换数字的位置。换言之，汉语中文不管多长的句子，一定都是没有①就没有②，没有①、②就没有③，没有①、②、③就没有④，没有①、②、③、④就没有⑤；以此类推，即先是什么，再是什么，接下去是什么，再接下去又是什么，一直到句末的核目词出现，才构成一个完整的句子。比如，英文句子

I will go to the college library to read books at 7 pm tomorrow evening.

按照英文的字序翻译成中文就是"①我②去③学校④图书馆⑤看⑥书⑦七点⑧明天⑨晚上。"

但是这句话在中文是不通的。因为英文①－⑨的词序不是实际生活步骤的纪实。设想真的一步一步按生活去做，并且有一架录像机去实录，它的顺序一定是：

① I，② tomorrow，③ in the evening，④ at 7 pm，⑤ will go to，⑥ the college，⑦ library，⑧ to read，⑨ books.

换成中文即："①我，②明天，③晚上，④七点，⑤去，⑥学校，⑦图书馆，⑧看，⑨书"。

没有①的"我"，②的"明天"就失去了意义。没有①＋②，"我明天"，③的"晚上"就是一个抽象的概念，因为实际生活是明天的子夜先来临，其后是清晨、早上、上午、中午、下午，才到这个特指的③"晚上"；同样的理由，没有①、②、③，④的"七点"也是一个泛指，只有在②、③"明天晚上"的制约下，④的"七点"才具有时间的含义。再往后的⑤"去"，没有①－④，即话语者如果不查看时间，他就不会有"去"的行为，即一定是"明天晚上七点"这个特定的时刻要"去"。接下去是⑥，这个人去的目标"学校"，先到了学校，才能到⑦的"图书馆"，进了图书馆，才能有机会阅读，即⑧的"看"。看什么？最后才触及在一连串时空行为后的核心目标⑨，看"书"。

这个句子存在着一个唯一的可变式，即①的"我"，与②的"明天"、③的"晚上"，以及④"七点"的对调。即：明天 晚上 七点 我 去 学校 图书馆 看 书。

这句话是于某种语境下，话语者告诉他人，从"明天晚上七点"这个时刻起要做的事情；而上一句话，话语者是从今天起计划要做的事情，即"我 明天 晚上 七点去 学校 图书馆 看 书。"

这个句子在序法的涵盖下，还有两点与英文不同：

一、字与词：英文的这句话由9个词和短语构成，但是中文是13个字。为什么？因为，②的"明天" tomorrow 在英文是一个词，在中文是两个字（tomorrow + sky）；④、⑤的"晚上"(evening + up) 也同样。相同的还有⑥的"学校"(study + educational establishment) 和由三个汉字组构成的"图书馆"(picture + book + building)。

二、句末的字词：英文句子最末的词是 evening（晚上），中文是"书"。由此可以知道，作为汉语，句子最末的一个字词出现之前，前面的行文都在提供时空的信息，唯有句末的核目词出现了，句义才明朗。试着把上面的核目词换成"王馆长"，即"我明天晚上七点去学校图书馆看王馆长。"在"王馆长"出现之前，由①－⑧都是信息，而英文则不是。

以上这个句子展现了汉语中文的"趋真向心"、渐进行文的特点，即句子越往后，越接近句子的核目词。因此，任何一位想学习汉语的人，只要按照他日常生活的顺序把汉语的单词植入即可，

如果他们这样做了，句子的核目词一定会出现在句末。反过来说，一个学习汉语的人在听汉语的时候，一定要把注意力集中在最后的一两个字词上。

可以用两句话来概括中文的序法："我口说我做，我手记我行。"

在这套《突破初 / 中 / 高级中文》教材里，第一步是采用四种方式帮助学习者记忆汉字：

一、用眼——看汉字衍化成的卡通画（见于初级上、下册和中级上册）；

二、用脑——拆解汉字，分析这个字组构所用的声符、义符等；

三、用耳朵——用一句上口的英文来帮助学生记忆汉字的形声；

四、用手——要求学生反复按笔顺书写汉字。

第二步，就是用第一步学会的汉字，加上运用汉语的序法（趋真向心的公式），把这些独体的汉字连成词、短语和句子，便成为一句标准的汉语了。当然，就像其他语言一样，文法的作用是使语言的表达言简意赅。汉语中也有不多的表达文法的语法字，通常使用的只有9个："的""地""得""了""着""过""吗""呢"和"吧"，以及没有实义的感叹词与拟声词。这些语法字很容易掌握，而且对初学者来说，没有那么重要。因为语法字的使用比例在文章中仅占4%左右，甚至可以说，汉语可以在完全没有这些语法字的情况下，凭着字词的排列顺序传达文义。

最后，我们希望这套语法体系不是"授人以鱼"，而是"授人以渔"。

Guide for Readers

Chinese characters play an important role for learners who want to learn Chinese seriously. Not knowing or being unable to write Chinese characters will affect learners' mastery of the language.

To take the HSK 1-3 exams as an example, learners who do not pay attention to Chinese characters and are only interested in using pinyin may pass the HSK Level 1-2 exams after a period of exclusively studying pinyin. But if they want to reach Level 3, they will find that the exam papers are all in Chinese characters and there is no pinyin. As a result, they will have to go right back to step one and learn Chinese characters.

Zoom In: Elementary Chinese in 60 Hours (and Intermediate Chinese in 118 Hours, Advanced Chinese in 337 Hours), is a set of learning materials suitable for both classes and self-learners. This textbook includes two parts and is accompanied by a workbook:

The first part (from Lesson 1 to Lesson 15) contains a total of 178 Chinese characters for practising writing, reading, speaking, and listening.

The second part (Lessons 16 to 30) uses these 178 Chinese characters to construct 1200 words and phrases as well as 890 sentences.

The workook includes exercises and a short novel. This novel uses the 178 characters studied in Part I as a base to create a story of some 3,000 Chinese characters. The way to unravel the story is to use the "Rolling Snowball" method. This consists of using the short stories and grammatical hints found in every Lesson from lessons 16 to 30 in Part II of the book in order to accumulate sufficient knowledge to read and understand the story.

The following instructions explain how to study Part I and Part II , and then how to proceed with the exercises in the workbook.

Part I

Each lesson (in total 15 lessons) in Part I contains 12 Chinese characters which each need to progress through 7 steps.

Take the word "love" numbered 001 from Lesson 1 as an example:

Lesson One 001-012 Meaning, Pronunciation & Tone

2   1

Radical/Component ⺶ fingers   爱（愛＊）LOVE ài | **001**

LOVE ài   爱 ——3

Traditional form 愛

⺶ (fingers) + ∩ ⼌ (roof) + 友 (friend) = love ——4

Catchphrase

Your friend must **LOVE** you very much if he is willing to lend you a hand with the construction of your house! **LOVE** is 爱 ài. ——5

Stroke order

丿 丷 爫 爫 爫 爫 ⺈ 冖 𡗗 𡗗 爱 ——6

The 7 steps are as follows：

1	The meaning, pronunciation and tone 字义和发音及声调
2	Radical / Component 偏旁部首
3	Cartoon 动画汉字
4	The divided combination 字的分解
5	The catchphrase 记字口诀
6	The stroke order 字的笔顺
7	Strictly follow the instructions for each exercise in the workbook. (The exercises are accompanied by recordings in English and standard Mandarin)

Note: do it step by step, don't jump.

1. The catchphrase in Step 5 serves as a mnemonic tip that tells the meaning of the character, partly through its pictographic origin going back thousands of years. At the end of the catchphrase is the meaning in English and the pronunciation and tone of the character.

2. When writing Chinese characters, one should use good horizontal and vertical strokes, and they should write in a special Chinese character notebook with squares; it is especially important to write characters by following the demonstrated stroke order on the page.

3. According to statistics, the average time required to remember a Chinese character is approximately 5 minutes. The book has a total of 178 characters, which thus takes 15 hours to complete.

Part II

The second part (Lessons 16 to 30): Once students have mastered the 178 Chinese characters, this part will help them to compose about 1,200 words, phrases and 890 sentences using the "Natural Order Method".

Take the first Chinese character, "love", which is again used in Lesson 16 (which covers a total of 12 Chinese characters) as an example.

Note: The character "love" has already appeared in Lesson 1 of the first part, in order to decode and memorize this character. In Lesson 16, this character is combined with other characters to form some words and phrases.

The table below shows that the character "love"can be combined to form at least 13 words or phrases, and five sentences. Whilst the first three sentences in bold are relatively simple and need to be studied, the last two sentences are longer, more complicated, and mainly tailored for learners with a strong language learning ability.

1. The left-hand column in the upper part of the table shows words or phrases constructed with the character "love". The audio recording is available at www.sinolingua.com.cn. The most efficient way to learn is to use the recording and the textbook at the same time, listening to each word or phrase and then repeating it. The middle column of the table gives the English equivalent. The right column of the table

shows the numbers corresponding to the Chinese characters that make up the words or phrases.

2. The lower part of the table shows sentences made with the character "love" and there are nine steps for learners to do:

1) Try to read the sentence; 2) Read it again; 3) Try to understand the meaning of the sentence; 4) Check the English provided for each sentence to make sure they understand it correctly; 5) Try to look at the English and retranslate the sentence back into Chinese; 6) Compare the sentence they translated with the original Chinese sentence; 7) Read the Chinese of the original sentence aloud again; 8) Listen to the recording of the sentence; 9) Follow the recording and read three or four times.

3. There are sometimes small "tips" next to the table. Do not ignore them.

Please take good use of the exercise section of each lesson in the workbook. In order to consolidate the knowledge learned, learners are advised to strictly follow the instructions.

The workbook also contains a novel which learners can read as a supplementary reading exercise. Learners can read the novel after they have studied Lesson 16. The novel is written using the "Rolling Snowball" method — one of the learning methods. Thus, in Lesson 16, the snowball has just begun to roll. As the learner's reading abilities gradually increase through the lessons, the snowball gets bigger and bigger until, by Lesson 30, a huge snowball has been accumulated which is a novel of some 3,000 Chinese characters.

There is a recording of the novel in standard Chinese that helps to train the learner's listening skills. This is an opportunity to listen to a professional reading. Of course, this story does not end here, and it will continue to unfold in the series.

Reading for Lesson 16-30

The names of people in this story

Full names	Surnames	Given names
钟天明	钟	天 - 明
谢小星	谢	小 - 星
高亮	高	亮

In China, full names are composed such that the surname of the family always comes first, before the given name.

Notes

1. Some characters are **in square and bold** : these are measure words.

2. Some characters are **in bold**: these are the grammatical codes.

3. Some characters are highlighted in grey with dotted key words: these are useful sentence patterns or phrases.

4. Some characters are underlined: these are proper nouns.

路在我们的脚下（第一部）（1—15 单篇注释版）

1

　　钟天明、谢小星和高亮，三 |个| 人是大学的同学。

　　钟天明是男（male nán）学生，个子很高，有一米八零。他爸爸是一 |个| 书商，在北京开了十几 |家| 书店①。

　　谢小星是一 |个| 很漂亮的女学生。她的爸爸是一 |家| 医院的医生，她妈妈在家，不工作②。

　　高亮是一 |个| 很爱看书的男（male nán）学生，他的学习很好。在大学，他是一 |个| 有名的好学生③。他的爸爸妈妈，一 |个| 是中学的老师，一 |个| 是小学的老师④。

　　钟天明、谢小星和高亮三 |个| 人是好朋友。

Grammatical Notes

① 他爸爸是一 |个|（measure word）书商，在北京开了（了 indicates the action that has been completed）十几 |家|（measure word）书店。

② 她妈妈在家，不工作 (Notice: the difference between 不工作 & 没工作；不工作 = don't want to work; 没工作 = do not have a job)。

③ 高亮是一 |个| 很爱看书的男学生 (In front of the grammatical code 的，there are three pieces of information about the male student: A. 一　个　=　one + the measure word; B. 很爱　=　very fond of...; C. 看书　=　reading books)……

④ 他（的）(When describing interpersonal relationship, normally the modifier 的 can be omitted with very close relatives.) 爸爸妈妈，一 |个| 是中学的老师，一 |个| 是小学的老师。

本书使用说明

一、本书对象

1. 完全没有汉语基础，从零开始学习的人。

2. 会说一些汉语，但是不认识汉字的人。

3. 对中国文字和文字文化感兴趣的人。

二、本书特点

1. 本书把汉语的发生、发展与成熟当作一个独特的历史现象，把汉字看作汉语的根本。为此，本书着重介绍汉字，让学习者在掌握汉字的同时逐步提高汉语听说读写的能力。

2. 本书以汉语的"序法"为总规则贯穿全书，不谈词性和结构，学习者不能以印欧语系的理念来套用汉语。

3. 全套书分6个级别，包括初级上、下册，中级上、下册和高级上、下册。

三、本书结构及使用说明

1. 本套教材既适于班级教授也适于自学使用，每个级别包括课本和练习册两本书。

初级课本（上册）共分30课，每课1小时，全书需要30小时完成。包括两部分：第一部分（第1至15课）是"字部"，共包含178个汉字的写、读、说和听；第二部分（第16至30课）是"词句部"，与前面"字部"所学的汉字对接，使用178个汉字去组构1200个词和短语和造890个句子。

初级练习册（上册）包括：1-30课练习；参考答案；拓展阅读（一篇长达3000个汉字、名为《路在我们的脚下》的小说，展开的方式是"滚雪球"）。

2. 初级课本（上册）第1至15课，是学习178个汉字的部分，每课包含12个汉字，以"爱"字为例：

a   b

Radical/Component ⩘ fingers　　爱（愛＊）LOVE ài　**001** —— c

—— d

LOVE ài　　*爱* —— e

Traditional form 愛

⩘（fingers）+ ⌂ （roof）+ 友（friend）= love —— f

Catchphrase

Your friend must **LOVE** you very much if he is willing to lend you a hand with the construction of your house! **LOVE** is 爱 ài. —— g

Stroke order

—— h

a) "爱"字的偏旁部首；

b) "爱"字的英文词义及拼音；

c) "爱"字在全书178个字中的编号001；

d) 看图识字；

e) "爱"字的英文字义、拼音与放大的汉字；

f) "爱"字的结构部件；

g) "爱"字的口诀，是记忆这个字形、声与调的英文；

h) "爱"字的笔顺。

3. 每个字的学习分7步，要一步一步进行，不可以跳跃：

1) The meaning, pronunciation and tone 字义和发音及声调
（b、e）；汉字是表义文字，大部分字只有一个音（少数字有多音），
汉语普通话的声调有四个，有的字读轻声。普通话全部发音加
上声调一共约1100个，比起其他语言非常有限。声调的调式
如右图：

线①是第一声，高起，保持高而平；线②是第二声，起于
中间，越往后越高；线③是第三声，先降到最低，然后上扬；
线④是第四声，起高，急速下降到底；轻声通常没有调式，发
音的时候要轻而短。

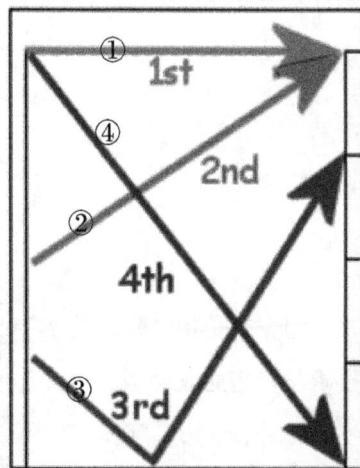

2) Radical / Component 偏旁部首 (a)。

3) Cartoon 动画汉字 (d)。

4) The divided combination 字的分解 (f)。

5) Catchphrase 记字口诀 (g)，通常是一个有趣的故事，一般是中国古人造字的依据，极少汉
字由于被简化等原因，口诀则采取以学生能一下子记住的方式来表述，口诀的最后是这个字的字
义与发音。

6) Stroke order 字的笔顺 (h)，要严格地按照书中的笔画顺序书写，笔画是从左往右、从上往下，
有些字是从中间一笔起始；笔画要横平竖直，并写在专用的汉字米字格本里。

7) 按照题目要求，完成练习册中相应的练习。

据统计，记忆一个汉字的平均时间是4–5分钟。全书178个汉字，共需要15个小时完成。

4. 第16课至第30课，在掌握了178个汉字的基础上，再把这些汉字按照"序法"组成1200个词、
短语和890个句子。如，"字部"第1课所学的12个汉字，在"词句部"的第16课里全部出现，
不同的是要用这12个汉字分别组构出词、短语和句子。仍以"爱"字为例（第1课的第1个字，
会再次出现在第16课，即词句部分的第1课中）：

词表左边一列，是用"爱"字组构的词或短语，课本提供了录音，边听边读是最好的方式。中间一列是对应的英文。右边一列是组成这个词或短语的汉字编号。如"爱"前构的词为"喜爱"be fond of，"爱"后构的词为"爱人"lover/partner。每字提供大约5-8个前构或后构的词或短语。

Chinese	English	Character codes
爱 + 人 爱人	love + people lover/partner	001/104
我 + 爱人 我爱人	my spouse	132/001/104
爱 + 国 爱国	love + country be patriotic	001/036
很爱国	be very patriotic	043/001/036
爱家	love + family love one's family	001/053
爱做	love + do love to do	001/178
爱做饭	love to cook food	001/178/026
爱喝	love + drink love to drink	001/041
爱喝茶	love to drink tea	001/041/009
爱漂亮	love + clean + bright love to be pretty	001/093/070
友爱	friend + love love/fraternity	157/001
喜爱	happy + love be fond of	137/001
关爱	care + love concern and care	034/001

句表则是用"爱"的本字及词或短语造出的句子。其中1、2、3句是比较简单的汉语句子，要求学习者必须掌握，字体加黑。4、5两个句子比较长，也相对复杂一些，可以根据学习者的情况决定是否学习，字体不加黑。1–5句都有英文译文供参照。标星号 * 的，有注释。

1/001	Chinese	他爱人是老师。*	
	English	His wife is a teacher.	
2/001	Chinese	爸爸妈妈很关爱我们。	
	English	Daddy and Mummy love and care for us.	
3/001	Chinese	他很喜爱他的狗。	
	English	He is very fond of his dog.	
4/001	Chinese	他爱喝茶和爱吃中国菜。**	
	English	He loves to drink tea and also loves to eat Chinese food.	
5/001	Chinese	A: 大家都去哪儿了？ B: 有一些人在那儿，有一些爱漂亮的人去商店买衣服了。	
	English	A: Where is everyone? B: Some of them are over there; some who love to be pretty have gone to the store to buy clothes.	

注释 Note

* 爱人 in terms of social relations only refers to a spouse, like wife or husband.
** 和 hé = and

使用顺序：首先学生试着读一遍；然后再读一遍；试着理解这个句子的句义；参照每句话提供的英文，检查否理解得正确；试着看着英文，把句子反过来翻译成中文；再对照英翻中的句子与原来的句子做比较；再把原句的中文大声念读一遍；最后聆听句子配套的普通话录音，随着录音再念读三至四遍。

5. 练习册前半部分是每课对应的练习，各有听说读写和翻译的习题，请严格依照指令去做。

6. 练习册后半部分是字词拓展内容，这是一篇叫《路在我们的脚下》的小说。小说以"滚雪球"

的学习方式展开，即，学习第 16 课时雪球刚刚开始滚，随着阅读能力的逐渐提高，雪球越滚越大，学到第 30 课时大雪球滚完——是一篇长达 3000 个汉字的小说。小说配有标准普通话录音（录音于 www.sinoling.com.cn 下载），这是一个聆听专业人士朗读这个有趣故事的机会。当然，这个故事并没有结束，它将在 2 级教材中继续滚下去。

三、本书预期的目标

1. 学习者经过 30 小时的学习，可以达到：有能力正确地书写 178 个汉字；有一般语言能力的学生可以听懂、阅读、说出和翻译 534 个句子，能力强或用功的学生可以阅读、翻译 890 个句子。

2. 学生获得古今汉字演变的知识，汉字的组构方式、汉语中词的组构方式，以及句子的"趋真向心"含义。

3. 为进入下一级——也就是初级中文（下册）——打下坚实的听说读写基础。

字篇

目录 Contents

词句篇

附录

字篇

Radical/Component ⧟ fingers 爱（愛*）LOVE ài | 001

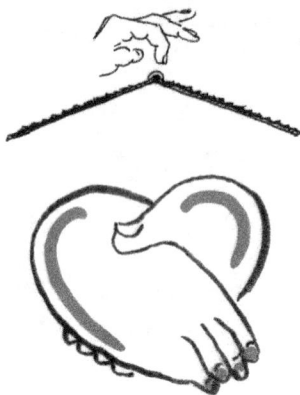

LOVE ài 爱

Traditional form 愛

⧟ （fingers）+ ⌂ 一（roof）+ 友（friend）= love

Catchphrase

Your friend must LOVE you very much if he is willing to lend you a hand with the construction of your house! LOVE is 爱 ài.

Stroke order

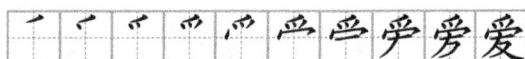

* 为便于各地区学生使用，如果这个汉字有繁体字，就在此处括弧内标明。

* The ancient forms of the character, if any, are included for the reader's reference through the textbook.

Radical/Component 八 eight/divide 八 EIGHT bā | 002

EIGHT bā 八

Ancient form)(

Catchphrase

A moustache looks like the number EIGHT in Chinese. EIGHT is 八 bā.

Stroke order

丿 八

Radical/Component 父 father 爸 DAD bà | 003

DAD bà 爸

父（holding two sharp weapons）+ 巴（snake-shaped reptile）= dad

Catchphrase

DAD will scare away the dangerous snakes with a pair of axes. DAD is 爸 bà.

Stroke order

| Radical/Component | 木 wood/tree | 杯 CUP/GLASS bēi | **004** |

CUP/GLASS bēi 杯

木（wood）+ 不（not/no）= cup/glass

Catchphrase

After some carving, it was no longer a piece of wood, but had turned into a CUP. CUP/GLASS is 杯 bēi.

Stroke order

一 十 才 才 木 朽 杯 杯

| Radical/Component | the first stroke of the character | 北 NORTH bēi | **005** |

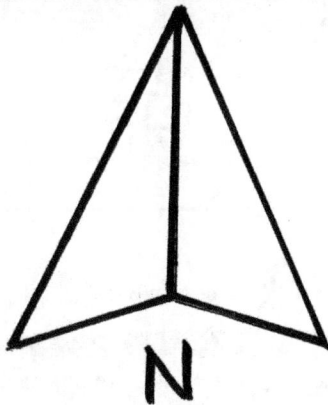

NORTH bēi 北

Ancient form 𠂆

Catchphrase

The paper plane is headed toward the NORTH Sea. NORTH is 北 bēi.

Stroke order

丨 十 扎 北 北

| Radical/Component 木 wood/tree | 本 ORIGIN/ROOT běn | **006** |

ORIGIN/ROOT běn 本

木（wood/tree）+ 一（base/ground）= origin/root

Catchphrase

A tree's ORIGIN is in its roots, essential for absorbing nutrients from the soil. ORIGIN/ROOT is 本 běn.

Stroke order

一 十 才 木 本

Radical/Component 一 the first stroke of the character 不 NOT/NO bù | 007

NOT/NO bù 不

一（sky）+ 🐦 (bird) = not/no

Catchphrase

When birds migrate, they will **NOT** be seen again until the following year. **NOT** is 不 bù.

Stroke order

一 ア 才 不

Radical/Component 艹 grass/flower/leaf 菜 VEGETABLE cài | 008

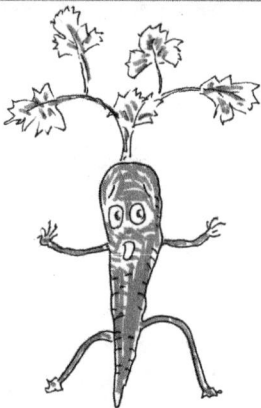

VEGETABLE cài 菜

Ancient form 𦬊

ψψ 艹（grass）+ 彐 (fingers)+ ✳ 木 (tree) = vegetables

Catchphrase

When **VEGETABLES** are ready to be eaten, farmers pick them by hand. **VEGETABLE** is 菜 cài.

Stroke order

一 十 艹 艹 艹 艺 艺 芯 苹 苹 菜 菜

Radical/Component 艹 grass/flower/leaf 茶 TEA chá | 009

TEA chá 茶

Ancient form 𣗵

ψψ 艹 (leaves) + 𠆢 人 (person) + ✳ 木 (tree)= tea

Catchphrase

To make **TEA**, workers carefully pluck the tops off tea bushes before processing and drying the leaves. **TEA** is 茶 chá.

Stroke order

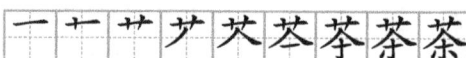

一 十 艹 艹 艾 苓 苓 茶 茶

| Radical/Component — the first stroke of the character | 车（車）VEHICLE chē | **010** |

VEHICLE chē 车

Traditional form 車

Catchphrase

This character represents a wheel. A unicycle only has one wheel, but it is still a **VEHICLE. VEHICLE is** 车 chē.

Stroke order

一 车 车 车

| Radical/Component 口 mouth | 吃 EAT chī | **011** |

EAT chī 吃

Ancient form 吃

口 口（mouth）+ 气 乞（kneeling down to beg）= eat

Catchphrase

This is to beg for something to EAT. **EAT is** 吃 chī.

Stroke order

丨 冂 口 叮 吃 吃

| Radical/Component 丨 vertical stroke | 出 EXIT chū | **012** |

EXIT chū 出

Ancient form 出

Catchphrase

The stems EXIT their buds. **EXIT is** 出 chū.

Stroke order

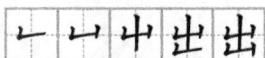
丄 凵 屮 出 出

Radical/Component 扌 hand | 打 STRIKE dǎ | **013**

STRIKE dǎ 打

Ancient form 𣏂

𣎳 扌（hand）+ 个 丁 (hammer) = to strike/hit/break

Catchphrase

A hammer in the hand is good for **STRIKING** nails into hard surfaces. **STRIKE** is 打 dǎ.

Stroke order

Radical/Component 大 big | 大 BIG dà | **014**

BIG dà 大

Ancient form 大

一 一 (stretched arms) + 𠂉 人 (person) = big

Catchphrase

The boy used a pump to stretch himself out like a balloon and make himself look **BIG**. **BIG** is 大 dà.

Stroke order

一 ナ 大

Radical/Component 白 white | 的 Grammatical Code de | **015**

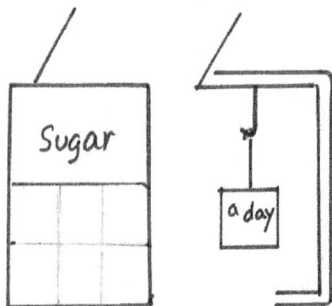

Grammatical Code de 的

Ancient form 睯

白 白（white sugar）+ 勺 勺 (spoon)=a particle used after an attributive

Catchphrase

LIMIT yourself to one spoon of sugar per day. The grammatical code used to limitation is 的 de.

Stroke order

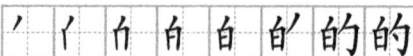

Radical/Component ⺣ fire 点（點）DROP diǎn **016**

DROP diǎn 点

Traditional form 點

占 (occupy; take) + ⺣ ⺀ (fire; drop) = drop; to order

Catchphrase

Four **DROPS** of chilli oil in your tomato soup will warm you up on a cold day. **DROP/ TO ORDER** is 点 diǎn.

Stroke order

丶	上	占	占	占	点	点	点	点

Radical/Component 田 field 电（電）ELECTRICITY diàn **017**

ELECTRICITY diàn 电

Traditional form 電

Catchphrase

A bolt of lightning full of **ELECTRICITY** struck an open field. **ELECTRICITY** is 电 diàn.

Stroke order

丨	冂	日	曰	电

Radical/Component 广 half roof 店 SHOP diàn **018**

SHOP diàn 店

广 (dotted cliff/half roof) + 占 (occupy; take) = shop; store; inn

Catchphrase

Many traditional, small **SHOPS** in China occupy a half-opened side of a house on a street. **SHOP** is 店 diàn.

Stroke order

丶	一	广	广	庀	庐	店	店

| Radical/Component — the first stroke of the character | 东（東）EAST dōng | **019** |

EAST dōng 东

Ancient form 🌳 Traditional form 東
日 (sun) + 木 (tree)= east

Catchphrase
The tree is blocking you from seeing the sun rise from the EAST. EAST is 东 dōng.

Stroke order

一 七 车 东 东

| Radical/Component 阝 city | 都 ALL dōu | **020** |

ALL dōu 都

Ancient form 都

堵 (land; people)+ 日 日 (sun) + 阝 阝 (city) = all/ both

Catchphrase
This city really has it ALL: land, people and the sun. ALL is 都 dōu.

Stroke order

一 十 土 耂 耂 者 者 者 都 都

| Radical/Component 讠 language | 读（讀）READ dú | **021** |

READ dú 读

Traditional form 讀

讠 讠 (language) + 卖 (sell) = to read/read aloud/study

Catchphrase
He READ many books about how to use convincing language to sell goods. READ is 读 dú.

Stroke order

ˋ 讠 讠 讠 讲 读 读 读 读 读

Radical/Component 又 hand   对（對）FACE duì | 022

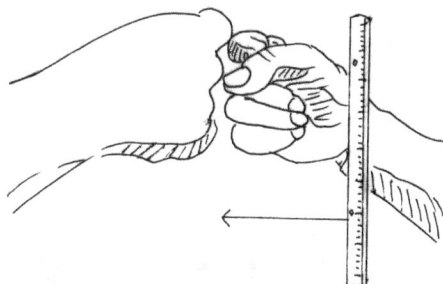

FACE duì   对

Traditional form 對

又（hand）+ 寸（tool）= toward/to face/to correct

Catchphrase

Before you FACE your opponent, you should size them up: measure them with your hand or a tool. FACE is 对 duì.

Stroke order

フ　又　对　对　对

Radical/Component 夕 twilight   多 MANY/MORE duō | 023

MANY/MORE duō   多

Ancient form

（夕 twilight）+ （夕 twilight）= many/much/more

Catchphrase

One moon in the sky is beautiful, but two would be one too MANY. MANY/MORE is 多 duō.

Stroke order

ノ　ク　タ　夕　多　多

Radical/Component 儿 son   儿（兒）SON ér | 024

SON ér   儿

Traditional form 兒

Catchphrase

The CHILD steadied himself with his arms. SON or CHILD is 儿 ér.

Stroke order

ノ　儿

Radical/Component 二 two   二 TWO èr   **025**

TWO èr   二

Ancient form 二

一（one）+ 一（one）= two

Catchphrase

The horizon of the earth is ONE line and the skyline is another. One plus one equals **TWO. TWO is** 二 **èr**.

Stroke order

Radical/Component 饣 food   饭（飯）FOOD/RICE fàn   **026**

FOOD/ RICE fàn   饭

Ancient form 𩚳   Traditional form 飯

饣（cooked rice）+ 反（backhand）= meal

Catchphrase

Humans used the miracle of fire to turn grain into edible FOOD. **FOOD/ RICE is** 饭 **fàn**.

Stroke order

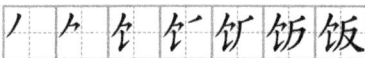

Radical/Component 乙 second   飞（飛）FLY fēi   **027**

FLY fēi   飞

Ancient form 乙   Traditional form 飛

Catchphrase

Birds flap their wings in order to **FLY. FLY is** 飞 **fēi**.

Stroke order

Radical/Component 八 eight/divide 分 DIVIDE fēn | 028

DIVIDE fēn 分

Ancient form 𠔻

)(八（a divided object）+ 丿 刀 (knife) = to separate/minute

Catchphrase

A sharp knife can be used to DIVIDE a bell pepper into two pieces. DIVIDE is 分 fēn.

Stroke order

丿 八 今 分

Radical/Component 月 boat/moon/organ 服 OBEY/SERVE fú | 029

OBEY/SERVE fú 服

Ancient form 𦚤

月 月（boat）+ 卩（slave）+ 又 又（force）= to obey/serve/dress/clothes

Catchphrase

Historically, slaves were forced onto boats and had to work hard and OBEY orders. OBEY is 服 fú.

Stroke order

丿 刀 月 月 月 服 服 服

Radical/Component 亠 lid 高 HIGH/TALL gāo | 030

HIGH/TALL gāo 高

Ancient form 髙

亠（roof/lid）+ 口（window）+ 冂（building/hall）+ 口（window）
= tall/high

Catchphrase

A TALL building has windows on many floors. TALL is 高 gāo.

Stroke order

丶 亠 亠 亠 古 古 高 高 高 高

Radical/Component 人 human   个（個）MW gè | **031**

MW gè 个

Traditional form 個

人（person）+ 丨 (one) = a general measure word which is placed between a number and an object

Catchphrase

One person is standing here: he MEASUREs the length of his body. The MEASURE WORD for a single object is 个 gè.

Stroke order

丿 个 个

Radical/Component 一 the first stroke of the character   工 WORK gōng | **032**

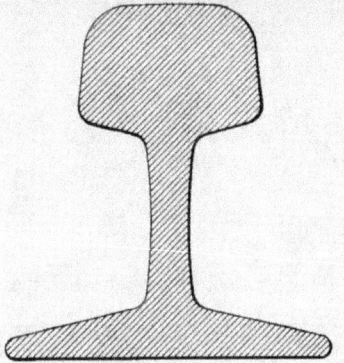

WORK gōng 工

Ancient form

Catchphrase

To make a strong iron rail requires hard WORK. WORK is 工 gōng.

Stroke order

一 丁 工

Radical/Component 犭 sharp teeth   狗 DOG gǒu | **033**

DOG gǒu 狗

Ancient form

犭 (animal with long and sharp teeth) + 句 (continued barking) = dog

Catchphrase

If you are afraid of DOGs, you may only notice their long, sharp teeth and loud bark. DOG is 狗 gǒu.

Stroke order

丿 犭 犭 犭 狗 狗 狗 狗

Radical/Component ⌄ hands/foot	关（關）SHUT/CLOSE guān	**034**

SHUT/CLOSE guān 关

Ancient form 𢇶   Traditional form 關

Catchphrase

A heavy window must be **SHUT** properly, using both hands. **SHUT/CLOSE** is 关 guān.

Stroke order

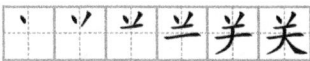

Radical/Component 饣 food	馆（館）BUILDING guǎn	**035**

BUILDING guǎn 馆

Ancient form 𩚛   Traditional form 館

食 饣（food）+ 𠆢（roof）+ 𠂤（official attire pattern）= building

Catchphrase

In ancient times, some **BUILDING**s were reserved for travelling officials to have somewhere to sleep and eat. **BUILDING** is 馆 guǎn.

Stroke order

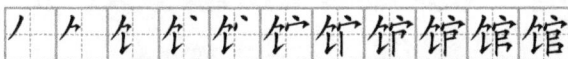

Radical/Component □ enclosure	国（國）COUNTRY guó	**036**

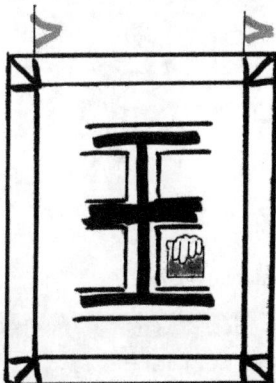

COUNTRY guó 国

Traditional form 國

口 口（city walls）+ 王 玉（king/jade）= country

Catchphrase

The city walls guard the emperor's precious jade seal, which is a symbol of the **COUNTRY**'s power and dignity. **COUNTRY/STATE** is 国 guó.

Stroke order

Radical/Component 木 wood/tree 果 FRUIT guǒ | 037

FRUIT guǒ 果

Ancient form 果

田 (farmland) + 木 (tree) = fruit

Catchphrase

FRUIT grows on trees just as crops grow in fields. FRUIT is 果 guǒ.

Stroke order

| 丨 | 冂 | 冃 | 日 | 旦 | 甲 | 果 | 果 |

Radical/Component 氵 river 汉（漢）HAN ETHNIC GROUP hàn | 038

HAN ETHNIC GROUP hàn 汉

Traditional form 漢

氵 (river/water) + 又 (again/repeat) = the Han ethnic group

Catchphrase

Over the centuries, the HAN people have suffered from the repeated flooding of their rivers. But at the same time they have built up strong willpower and the character for HAN is 汉 hàn.

Stroke order

| 丶 | 冫 | 氵 | 汈 | 汉 |

Radical/Component 女 woman 好 GOOD hǎo | 039

GOOD hǎo 好

Ancient form 好

女（woman）+ 子 (children) = good

Catchphrase

A mother and child usually have a GOOD relationship. GOOD is 好 hǎo.

Stroke order

| 乚 | 女 | 女 | 奵 | 好 | 好 |

Radical/Component 口 mouth   号（號）TRUMPET/DATE hào   040

TRUMPET/DATE hào   号

Traditional form 號

凵 口 (mouth) + ㇂ (musical instrument) = trumpet/date/number

Catchphrase

In ancient military camps, the sound of a TRUMPET in the very early morning always indicated a new day was starting. TRUMPET/DATE is 号 hào.

Stroke order

Radical/Component 口 mouth   喝 DRINK hē   041

DRINK hē   喝

Ancient form 喝

凵 口 (mouth) + 曷 (open mouth wide) = drink

Catchphrase

DRINKING too much water can stretch our stomachs! DRINK is 喝 hē.

Stroke order

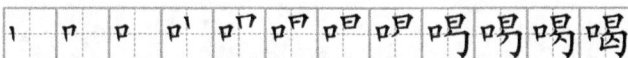

Radical/Component 口 mouth   和 HARMONY/PEACE/AND hé   042

HARMONY/ PEACE/AND hé   和

Ancient form 和

禾 (crops/cereals) + 凵 口 (mouth) = harmony/peace

Catchphrase

When the harvest is good, mouths are fed and HARMONY ensues in the community. HARMONY/PEACE /AND is 和 hé.

Stroke order

Radical/Component 彳 human activities/street　很 VERY hěn　043

VERY hěn 很

Ancient form 很

彳 (street) + 艮 (looks back) = very/very much/quite

Catchphrase

Crossing the street in heavy traffic can be **VERY** difficult, especially in Beijing! VERY is 很 hěn.

Stroke order

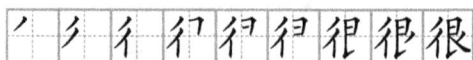

Radical/Component 口 mouth　后（後）BEHIND hòu　044

BEHIND hòu 后

The ancient form 后　Traditional form 後

（pregnant woman）+ 口（the mouth of a new born baby）= behind/next

Catchphrase

Children like to follow closely **BEHIND** their mothers. BEHIND is 后 hòu.

Stroke order

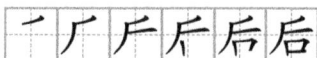

Radical/Component 亻 man　候 WAIT hòu　045

WAIT hòu 候

Ancient form 候

亻 (human) + 厂 (cliff) + 矢 (arrow) = wait

Catchphrase

The archers **WAIT** patiently by the cliff, arrows at the ready. WAIT is 候 hòu.

Stroke order

Radical/Component 讠 language 话（話）SPEECH/WORDS huà | **046**

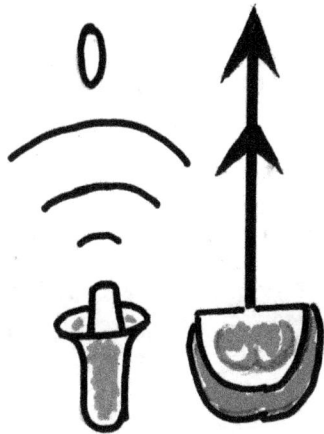

SPEECH/WORDS huà 话

The ancient form 舌 Traditional form 話

讠 (language/words) + 舌 (tongue) = speech/words

Catchphrase

SPEECH can sometimes wound more than a weapon! SPEECH/WORDS is 话 huà.

Stroke order

丶 讠 讠 计 计 计 话 话

Radical/Component 又 hand 欢（歡）WELCOME/JOYFUL huān | **047**

WELCOME/ JOYFUL huān 欢

Traditional form 歡

又 (waving arms) + 欠 (be out of breath/be exhausted) = welcome/joyful

Catchphrase

The family waved to us to WELCOME us home. JOYFUL is 欢 huān.

Stroke order

フ 又 ヌ 对 欢 欢

Radical/Component 囗 mouth 回 RETURN huí | **048**

RETURN huí 回

Ancient form 6

Catchphrase

To go home is to RETURN to one's roots. RETURN is 回 huí.

Stroke order

丨 冂 冂 回 回 回

Radical/Component 人 human	会（會）MEETING huì	**049**

MEETING huì 会

Traditional form 會

◇ (mouth talking) + ◟ 云 (cloud) = meeting

Catchphrase
If you see two rain clouds MEETING, there may soon be a downpour. MEETING is 会 huì.

Stroke order

Radical/Component 火 fire/anger	火 FIRE huǒ	**050**

FIRE huǒ 火

Ancient form 🔥

🔥 (flame) + 人 人 (person) = fire

Catchphrase
A flame is the visible part of a FIRE. FIRE is 火 huǒ.

Stroke order

Radical/Component 木 wood/tree	机（機）MACHINE jī	**051**

MACHINE jī 机

Traditional form 機

木 木 (wood/tree) + 几 几 (a simple wood tool) = machine

Catchphrase
Thousands of years ago, MACHINEs were all made from wood. MACHINE is 机 jī.

Stroke order

Radical/Component ノ the first stroke of the character 　　　几（幾）HOW MANY/FEW jǐ | **052**

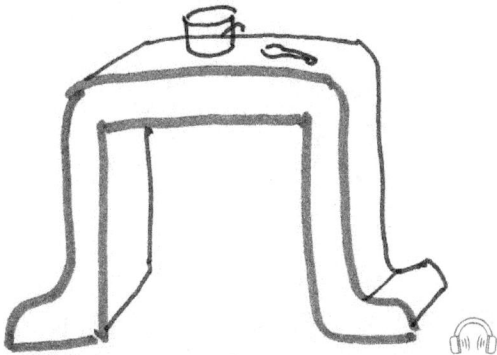

HOW MANY/ FEW jǐ 　几

Ancient form ∏　Traditional form 幾

Catchphrase

Q: **HOW MANY** pieces of wood to make this tea table?
A: A **FEW**.
HOW MANY/FEW is 几 jǐ.

Stroke order

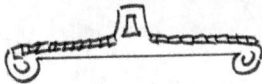

Radical/Component 宀 roof 　　　家 HOME/FAMILY jiā | **053**

HOME/ FAMILY jiā 　家

Ancient form 家

∩ 宀 (roof) + 丬 豕 (pig) = home

Catchphrase

In olden days, farmers kept their pigs inside their **HOMEs**. **HOME/FAMILY** is 家 jiā.

Stroke order

Radical/Component 见 see/meet 　　　见（見）SEE jiàn | **054**

SEE jiàn 　见

Ancient form 見　Traditional form 見

目 (eyes) + 儿 人 (body with two long legs) = see

Catchphrase

The ant's eyes are high on its head so that it can **SEE** farther. **SEE** is 见 jiàn.

Stroke order

Radical/Component 口 mouth　叫 YELL/SHOUT jiào　**055**

YELL/ SHOUT jiào　叫

Ancient form

ㅂ 口 (mouth) + ㇆ (using energy) = shout/yell

Catchphrase

Teachers use loudspeakers when **YELLING** at children in the schoolyard. **YELL/ SHOUT** is 叫 jiào.

Stroke order

丨 丨丨 口 叫 叫

Radical/Component 见 see/meet　觉（覺）SLEEP jiào; SENSE/FEEL jué　**056**

SLEEP jiào; SENSE/FEEL jué　觉

Traditional form 覺

(gain knowledge) + 见 (see/meet) = sleep/sense/feel

Catchphrase

When we **SLEEP**, our dreams can often offer us the best insights, inspiration and creativity. **SLEEP** is 觉 jiào.

Stroke order

丶 丶 丷 丷 丷 丷 常 觉 觉

Radical/Component 女 woman　姐 OLDER SISTER jiě　**057**

OLDER SISTER jiě　姐

Ancient form

女 (woman) + 且 (add/ladder) = elder sister

Catchphrase

The right side of this character is a ladder, which indicates the age gaps between the **ELDER SISTER** and younger sister in a family. **OLDER SISTER** is 姐 jiě.

Stroke order

乚 女 女 刘 如 如 姐 姐

Radical/Component 人 person   今 TODAY jīn   **058**

TODAY jīn 今

Ancient form

A (open mouth and tongue)+ — (wine) = today/present

Catchphrase

The cuckoo clock woke me up at 8:35 am **TODAY**. **TODAY/PRESENT** is 今 jīn.

Stroke order

ノ 人 亽 今

Radical/Component ⼇ lid/the top of a building   京 CAPITAL jīng   **059**

CAPITAL jīng 京

Ancient form

合 (temple/religion)+ 爪 (city gate) = capital

Catchphrase

A temple on top of a city wall usually denotes a gateway to the **CAPITAL**. **CAPITAL** is 京 jīng.

Stroke order

丶 一 亠 ⼗ 卢 宁 亨 京

Radical/Component ノ left falling stroke   九 NINE jiǔ   **060**

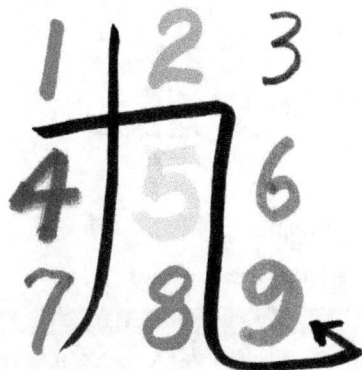

NINE jiǔ 九

Ancient form

Catchphrase

There is not too much difference between the character of FEW and the number of **NINE**. **NINE** is 九 jiǔ.

Stroke order

ノ 九

Radical/Component 一 the first stroke of the character 开（開）OPEN kāi | 061

OPEN kāi 开

Traditional form 開

— 一 (door bolt) + ㄠㄚ (two hands) = open

Catchphrase

When you OPEN a glass door, you must use both hands to balance the frame of the door, otherwise it will come off the rail. OPEN is 开 kāi.

Stroke order

一 二 干 开

Radical/Component 目 eyes 看 LOOK kàn | 062

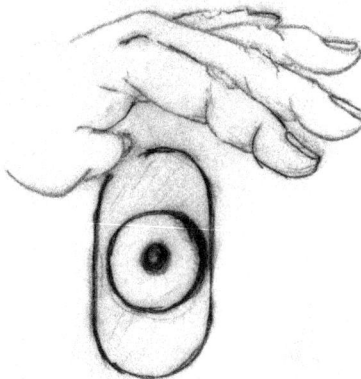

LOOK kàn 看

Ancient form 看

手 手（hand）+ 目 目 (eye) = watch/look

Catchphrase

Blocking the sun's glare with one hand enables one to SEE better on a bright day. LOOK/SEE is 看 kàn.

Stroke order

一 二 三 手 手 看 看 看 看

Radical/Component 宀 roof 客 GUEST kè | 063

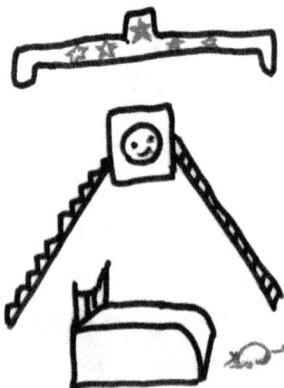

GUEST kè 客

Ancient form 客

宀 宀（roof）+ 各 各 (each/individual) = guests

Catchphrase

A tiny rat GUEST has arrived and wants to stay at this chalet-style hotel. GUEST is 客 kè.

Stroke order

丶 丷 宀 宀 宀 安 安 客 客

Radical/Component 土 soil/land   块（塊）PIECE kuài | **064**

PIECE kuài 块

Traditional form 塊

土 土（soil）+ 🏺 (pottery) = piece

Catchphrase
Clay jars are beautiful, but you must be careful not to drop them: they will smash into tiny PIECES. PIECE is 块 kuài.

Stroke order

一 十 土 圵 圵 块 块

Radical/Component 一 the first stroke of the character   来（來）COME lái | **065**

COME lái 来

Ancient form 𣏟   Traditional form 來

从（people）+ 木 (wood) = come

Catchphrase
A giant tree stretches out its branches to welCOME children to climb it. COME is 来 lái.

Stroke order

一 一 丆 立 平 来 来

Radical/Component 老 old   老 OLD lǎo | **066**

OLD lǎo 老

Ancient form 𦫳

𦫳 (bearded person) + 匕 (tool) = old

Catchphrase
A very OLD man may need a cane or a wheelchair to get around. OLD is 老 lǎo.

Stroke order

一 十 土 耂 老 老

IS OVER le　了

Ancient form 了

Catchphrase

When a baby boy is born, his time inside his mother's womb **IS OVER**. His life has begun. **IS OVER** is 了 le.

Stroke order

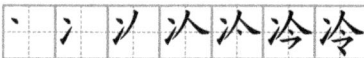

COLD lěng　冷

Ancient form 冷

冫（ice）＋ 令 (order/commander) = cold

Catchphrase

The Ice Queen, commander of the winter, has announced the **COLD** season is coming. **COLD** is 冷 lěng.

Stroke order

IN/INSIDE/CHINESE MILE lǐ　里

Ancient form 里　　Traditional form 裡

田（field）＋ 土 (soil) = in

Catchphrase

All things **IN** my farm belong to me. **IN** is 里 lǐ.

Stroke order

Radical/Component 亠 lid　亮 BRIGHT liàng　070

BRIGHT liàng 亮

Ancient form 亮

Catchphrase

The lighthouse shines **BRIGHTLY** over the sea at night. BRIGHT is 亮 liàng.

Stroke order

`丶 一 亠 产 产 产 亭 亭 亮`

Radical/Component 雨 rain　零 ZERO líng　071

ZERO líng 零 *

Ancient form 雨

雨（rain）+ 令 (order) = zero

Catchphrase

If the gods in the sky didn't order any rain to fall on the fields, we would have **ZERO** crops to harvest in the autumn. ZERO is 零 líng.

Stroke order

`一 厂 厂 币 币 币 雨 雨 雪 雰 雰 零 零`

* 二级词。

Radical/Component 亠 lid　六 SIX liù　072

SIX liù 六

Ancient form 六

Catchphrase

When we saw a candle in the shape of a "**SIX**" for his birthday, we felt happy. SIX is 六 liù.

Stroke order

`丶 一 广 六`

Radical/Component 口 mouth   吗（嗎）Question Code ma | **073**

Question Code ma 吗

Traditional form 嗎

口（mouth）+ 马（horse）= a question code

Catchphrase

I heard the **QUESTION** straight from the horse's mouth, so to speak. **Question Code** is 吗 ma.

Stroke order

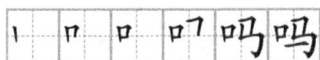

Radical/Component 女 woman   妈（媽）MUM mā | **074**

MUM mā 妈

Traditional form 媽

女 (woman) + 马 (horse) = mummy

Catchphrase

This female horse is **MUM** to everyone in the farming field. **MUM** is 妈 mā.

Stroke order

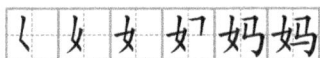

Radical/Component 乛 hook   买（買）BUY mǎi | **075**

BUY mǎi 买

Traditional form 買

乛 (hook) + 头 (head) = buy

Catchphrase

When people **BUY** goods in China, they typically haggle with the vendor to get a better price. **BUY** is 买 mǎi.

Stroke order

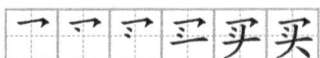

CAT māo　猫

Traditional form 貓

犭（animal with teeth or beard）+ 苗（meow sound）= cat

Catchphrase

A **CAT** may seem sweet with its meow and soft fur, but be careful of its sharp teeth! **CAT is** 猫 māo.

Stroke order

丿　犭　犭　犷　犴　犵　犵　猫　猫　猫　猫

WHAT SUFFIX me　么

Traditional form 麼

丿 + 厶（private）= what suffix

Catchphrase

For **WHAT** purpose is the boy kneeling on the floor? **WHAT SUFFIX is** 么 me.

Stroke order

丿　么　么

DISAPPEAR méi　没

Ancient form

水 氵 (river) + 儿 (whirlpool) + 又 (hand)= disappear

Catchphrase

The man reached out his hand before he **DISAPPEAR**ed down the whirlpool in the river. **DISAPPEAR is** 没 méi.

Stroke order

丶　冫　氵　氵　沕　没　没

Radical/Component ⺅ human 们（們）PLURAL FOR MANKIND men **079**

PLURAL FOR MANKIND men 们

Traditional form 們

⺅ 亻 (man) + 门 门 (door) = plural for mankind

Catchphrase

SEVERAL PEOPLE live behind these doors. PLURAL FOR MANKIND is 们 men.

Stroke order

丿 亻 亻 仃 们

Radical/Component 米 rice 米 RICE mǐ **080**

RICE mǐ 米

Ancient form ⺤

木（plant）+ ⺷（grains）= rice

Catchphrase

The Union Jack looks just like the Chinese character for RICE. RICE is 米 mǐ.

Stroke order

丶 丷 兰 半 米 米

Radical/Component ― the first stroke of the character 面 FACE miàn **081**

FACE miàn 面

Ancient form 圙

首 (hairs and nose) + 冂 (the shape of a face) = face

Catchphrase

This person's FACE resembles a pumpkin! FACE is 面 miàn.

Stroke order

一 丆 丆 而 而 面 面 面

Radical/Component 口 mouth 名 NAME míng | 082

NAME míng 名

Ancient form 名

ア 夕 (dark night) + 🔲 口 (open mouth) = name

Catchphrase

On a dark evening, people need to call each other's NAMES in order to locate one another. NAME is 名 míng.

Stroke order

ノ	ク	タ	タ	名	名

Radical/Component 日 sun 明 BRIGHT/TOMORROW míng | 083

BRIGHT/ TOMORROW míng 明

Ancient form 明

☉ 日 (sun) + 🌙 月 (moon) = bright

Catchphrase

If you see the moon in the sky while the sun is still out it means the sky TOMORROW will be BRIGHT. BRIGHT/TOMORROW is 明 míng.

Stroke order

l	冂	円	日	昒	明	明	明

Radical/Component 口 mouth 哪 WHERE/WHICH nǎ; něi | 084

WHERE WHICH nǎ; něi 哪

口 (open mouth) + 朿 (trees/bushes) + 阝 (town) = question word WHERE

Catchphrase

Here are the woods, but WHERE is the town centre? WHERE/WHICH is 哪 nǎ/něi.

Stroke order

l	口	口	叮	叼	吋	叩	明	哪	哪

Radical/Component 阝 town/city 那 THAT nà; nĕi 085

THAT nà; nèi 那

Ancient form

(trees/bushes) + 阝 (town) = that

Catchphrase

THAT city would be a lovely place to live in: it has many trees, large gardens, good transport and a beautiful lake. THAT is 那 nà/nĕi.

Stroke order

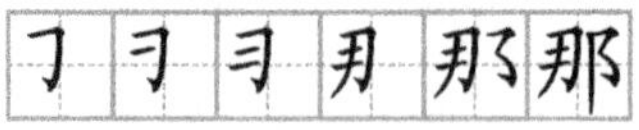

Radical/Component 月 moon/organ 脑（腦）BRAIN nǎo 086

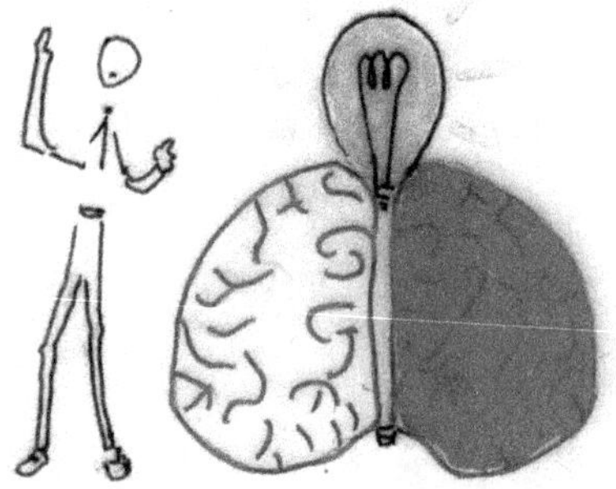

BRAIN nǎo 脑

Ancient form Traditional form 腦

月 (moon/radical for an organ) + (the shape of the brain) = brain

Catchphrase

The BRAIN is the organ that commands the human body. BRAIN is 脑 nǎo.

Stroke order

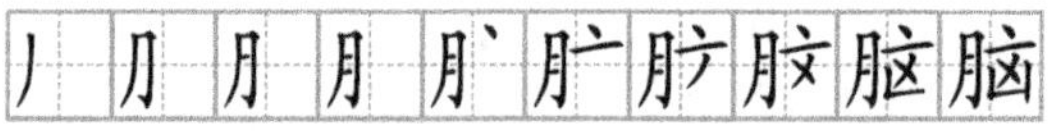

Radical/Component 口 mouth 呢 Question Code ne 087

Question Code ne 呢

口 (mouth) + (adult's chest) + (baby) = a follow-up question code

Catchphrase

Father: How are you, my baby? Baby: I am well, and you? The FOLLOW-UP Question Code after you is 呢 ne.

Stroke order

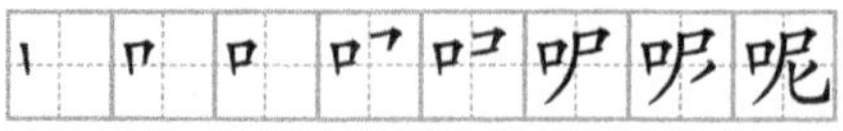

Radical/Component 厶 private 能 ABILITY néng **088**

ABILITY néng 能

Ancient form 熊

身 (body and head) + ⺇ (claws) = capability

🎧 🗣️ **Catchphrase**
A bear has the ABILITY to kill another animal with its sharp claws. ABILITY is 能 néng.

Stroke order

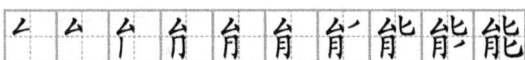

Radical/Component 亻 human 你 YOU nǐ **089**

YOU nǐ 你

Ancient form 尔

人 (man) + 尔 (arrows) = you

🎧 🗣️ **Catchphrase**
Cupid aimed an arrow at your heart and you fell in love with the next woman YOU saw. YOU is 你 nǐ.

Stroke order

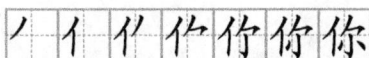

Radical/Component 丿 the first stroke of the character 年 YEAR nián **090**

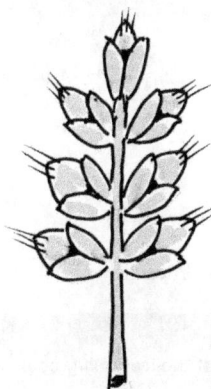

YEAR nián 年

Ancient form 秂

🎧 🗣️ **Catchphrase**
Once a YEAR, we harvest the wheat. YEAR is 年 nián.

Stroke order

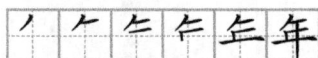

Radical/Component 女 woman 　　**女 WOMAN nǚ** | **091**

WOMAN nǚ 　女

Ancient form ᕗ

Catchphrase

This figure looks like a **WOMAN** sitting crossed-legged in a yoga pose! **WOMAN** is 女 nǚ.

Stroke order

Radical/Component 月 body/moon 　　**朋 FRIEND péng** | **092**

FRIEND péng 　朋

Ancient form
月(body) + 月(body) = friend

Catchphrase

Are they twins? Yes, and they are also **FRIENDS**. **FRIEND** is 朋 péng.

Stroke order

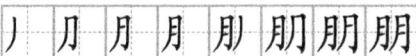

Radical/Component 氵 water/river 　　**漂 FLOATING piāo; BEAUTIFUL piào** | **093**

FLOATING piāo;
BEAUTIFUL piào 　漂

Ancient form
氵(water) + 票(float/ticket) = beautiful/floating

Catchphrase

The cat looked **BEAUTIFUL FLOATING** on the surface of the swimming pool. **BEAUTIFUL** is 漂 piào; **FLOATING** is piāo.

Stroke order

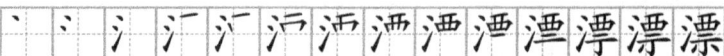

| Radical/Component ⁺⁺ grass/leaves | 苹（蘋）APPLE píng | **094** |

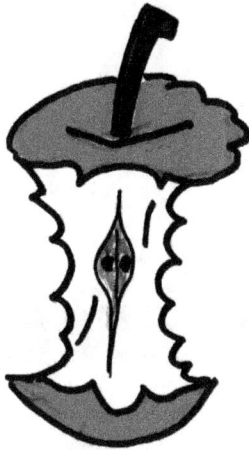

APPLE píng 苹

Tradition from 蘋
⁺⁺（leaves）+ 平 (peace/balance) = apple

Catchphrase

After you've eaten an APPLE to the core, all that is left is the leaves at the top and some seeds in the middle. APPLE is 苹 píng.

Stroke order

一 十 卄 艹 芇 芇 苹 苹 苹

| Radical/Component — The first stroke of the character | 七 SEVEN qī | **095** |

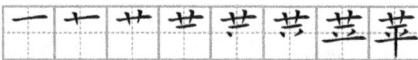
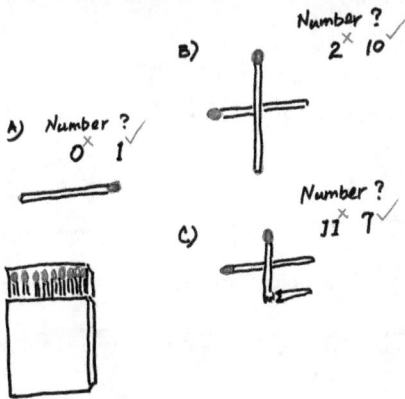

SEVEN qī 七

Ancient form 十

Catchphrase

The number SEVEN written in Chinese looks like the character for "ten" but with a bent leg. SEVEN is 七 qī.

Stroke order

一 七

| Radical/Component 月 moon/month/body | 期 PERIOD qī | **096** |

PERIOD qī 期

Ancient form 𦰩
其 (basket) + 月 (monthly) = period/hope

Catchphrase

I promised to deliver a basket of food to my family PERIODically. PERIOD is 期 qī.

Stroke order

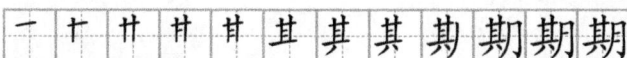

一 十 卄 廿 甘 甘 其 其 其 期 期 期 期

Radical/Component 走 walking | 起 LIFT/RISE qǐ | **097**

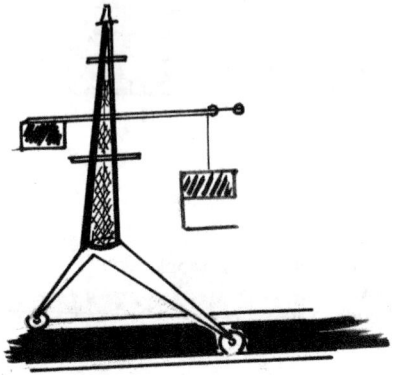

LIFT/RISE qǐ 起

Ancient form

走 (walk/move) + 已 (oneself) = lift/rise

Catchphrase

Lifting and holding a heavy container to move is a big job. **LIFT/RISE** is 起 qǐ.

Stroke order

一 十 土 キ キ キ 走 走 起 起 起

Radical/Component 气 air/gas | 气（氣）AIR qì | **098**

AIR qì 气

Ancient form 气 Traditional form 氣

Catchphrase

AIR is constantly flowing and in motion. **AIR** is 气 qì.

Stroke order

丿 ニ 气 气

Radical/Component ⺌ foot | 前 FRONT qián | **099**

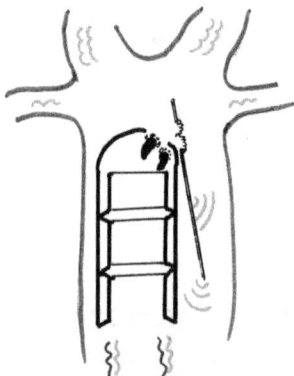

FRONT qián 前

Ancient form

彳 (cross junction) + ⺌ (foot) + 舟 (boat)= ahead/front

Catchphrase

That man is standing at the **FRONT** of his boat in order to guide it forward. **FRONT** is 前 qián.

Stroke order

丶 丷 丷 ソ 广 前 前 前 前 前

| Radical/Component 钅 metal | 钱（錢）MONEY qián | **100** |

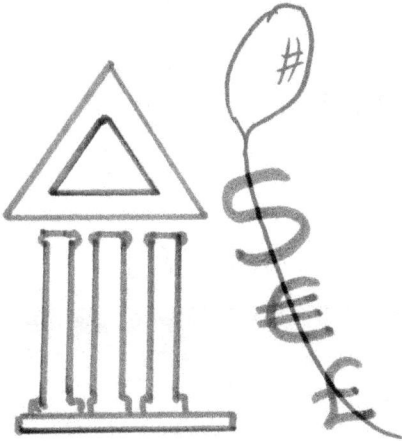

MONEY qián 钱

Ancient form 鐱 Traditional form 錢

金 钅（gold/metal）+ 戋（linked things）= currency/copper coin/money

Catchphrase

Using metal coins strung together was a popular form of CURRENCY in many countries. CURRENCY/ MONEY is 钱 qián.

Stroke order

丿 亻 𠂉 钅 钅 钅 钅 钱 钱 钱

| Radical/Component 讠 language | 请（請）PLEASE qǐng | **101** |

PLEASE qǐng 请

Ancient form 請 Traditional form 請

讠（language）+ 青（energy/young/green）= please; invite

Catchphrase

It is useful to say PLEASE with a lot of energy when requesting something in order to get a good result. PLEASE is 请 qǐng.

Stroke order

丶 讠 讠 讠 请 请 请 请 请

| Radical/Component 厶 private | 去 LEAVE/GO qù | **102** |

LEAVE/GO qù 去

Ancient form 去

𠓛（two people back to back）+ 厶 (private/mouth) = leave; go

Catchphrase

When a couple have trouble and argue a lot, one of them will eventually LEAVE! LEAVE/GO is 去 qù.

Stroke order

一 十 土 去 去

Radical/Component ⺮ fire 热（熱）HEAT rè **103**

HEAT rè 热

Traditional form 熱

🌿 (flame) + 丸 (body posture) = heat/hot

Catchphrase
In ancient times, people who lived in caves had to rely on HEAT from fires to stay warm. HEAT is 热 rè.

Stroke order

一 十 扌 扛 执 执 热 热 热 热

Radical/Component 人 people 人 PEOPLE rén **104**

PEOPLE rén 人

Ancient form 𠂉

Catchphrase
Most PEOPLE are always rushing around, seldom stopping to smell the roses. PEOPLE is 人 rén.

Stroke order

丿 人

Radical/Component 讠 language 认（認）RECOGNISE rèn **105**

RECOGNISE rèn 认

Traditional form 認

讠（language）+ 人（people）= know; recognise

Catchphrase
Hey man, I don't RECOGNISE the language you are reading! RECOGNISE is 认 rèn.

Stroke order

丶 讠 认 认

Radical/Component — the first stroke of the character   三 THREE sān | 106

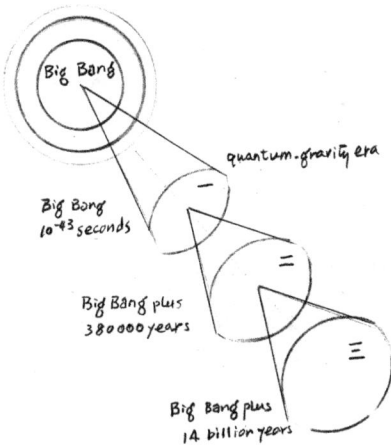

THREE sān 三

Ancient form 三

Catchphrase

One is heaven, two is earth, THREE is the human being who was created by the interaction between heaven and earth. THREE is 三 sān.

Stroke order

一 二 三

Radical/Component ⼇ lid/roof   商 TRADE shāng | 107

TRADE shāng 商

Ancient form 商

商 (an advertisement) + 冂 (meeting room) = commercial business/discuss

Catchphrase

Businessmen meet to discuss advertising and TRADE. TRADE is 商 shāng.

Stroke order

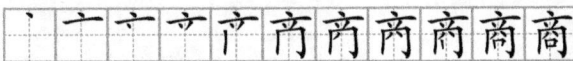

Radical/Component | the first stroke of the character   上 UP shàng | 108

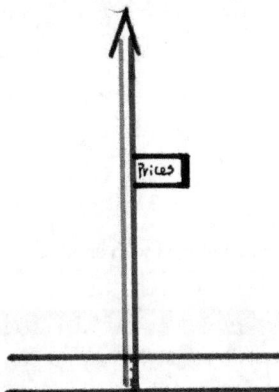

UP shàng 上

Ancient form 上

Catchphrase

A tall building rises UP from the ground towards heaven. UP is 上 shàng.

Stroke order

丨 上 上

| Radical/Component 小 small | 少 FEW shǎo; YOUNG shǎo | 109 |

FEW shǎo; YOUNG shǎo　少

Ancient form 小

Catchphrase

There seems to be too FEW beans to go around the table! FEW is 少 shǎo.

Stroke order

丨 ⺌ 小 少

| Radical/Component 讠 language | 谁（誰）WHO shuí; shéi | 110 |

WHO shuí; shéi　谁

Ancient form 𧧻　　Traditional form 誰

𧤭 讠(language) + 𨾊 (bird) = who

Catchphrase

WHO understands bird language? WHO is 谁 shéi.

Stroke order

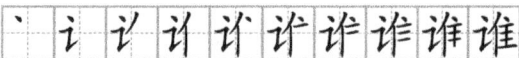

丶 讠 让 讠 让 计 谁 谁 谁 谁

| Radical/Component 亻 human | 什 WHAT shén | 111 |

WHAT shén　什

Ancient form 什

刀 亻（human） + 十 十 (ten) = what（often combined with another character）

Catchphrase

WHAT? You have ten questions to ask me! The first character in WHAT is 什 shén.

Stroke order

丿 亻 仁 什

| Radical/Component ノ the first stroke of the character | 生 BORN shēng | **112** |

BORN shēng 生

Ancient form ↓

↓ (bud/sprout) + ⬛ 一 (land) = born/give birth/produce

Catchphrase

A little bud grows out of the soil the same way a baby is BORN out of its mother's womb. BORN is 生 shēng.

Stroke order

ノ ᅡ ᅡ 牛 生

| Radical/Component 巾 scarf | 师（師）TEACHER shī | **113** |

TEACHER shī 师

Ancient form 𠂤帀   Traditional form 師

Catchphrase

This TEACHER is pointing out the answer to students. TEACHER is 师 shī.

Stroke order

丨 リ リ 师 师 师 师

| Radical/Component 一 the first stroke of the character | 十 TEN shí | **114** |

TEN shí 十

Ancient form ✝

Catchphrase

When counting, our ancestors would tie a knot for every TEN count. TEN is 十 shí.

Stroke order

一 十

Radical/Component 日 sun 　时（時）TIME shí | 115

TIME shí 时

Traditional form 時

⊟ 日（sun/sunlight）+ 寸（measure）= time

Catchphrase

People used to tell TIME by measuring the arc of the shadow on the sundial. TIME is 时 shí.

Stroke order

丨	冂	冂	日	日一	时	时

Radical/Component 讠 language 　识（識）KNOWLEDGE shí | 116

KNOWLEDGE shí 识

Traditional form 識

讠(language)+ 只（a single glass /only）= knowledge; recognise

Catchphrase

Words alone without the backing of real KNOWLEDGE are like bubbles without substance. KNOWLEDGE is 识 shí.

Stroke order

丶	讠	讠	识	识	识	识

Radical/Component 礻 spirit/religion 　视（視）SEE/LOOK shì | 117

SEE/LOOK shì 视

Ancient form 　Traditional form 視

礻 (the message of heaven) + 见 (stand and look) = vision/see/look

Catchphrase

To have insight into the workings of nature is to SEE properly. SEE/LOOK is 视 shì.

Stroke order

丶	亍	礻	礻	礻	礻	视	视

Radical/Component 日 sun　　是 TO BE/YES shì　**118**

TO BE/YES shì　是

Ancient form 昰

⊙ 日 (sun) + 疋 正 (foot/upright) = to be; correct; right; to be just right

Catchphrase

When the sun is overhead at midday, people pause to contemplate its positive energy and say 'YES' to life. **TO BE/YES** is 是 shì.

Stroke order

丨 冂 冂 日 旦 早 旱 昂 是

Radical/Component 一 hook　　书（書）BOOK shū　**119**

BOOK shū　书

Ancient form 書　Traditional form 書

乛 (hand) + 木 (brush) + 口 (inkstone) = to write

Catchphrase

You must use a brush soaked in ink to write a **BOOK** by hand. **BOOK** is 书 shū.

Stroke order

乛 乛 书 书

Radical/Component 水 river/water　　水 WATER shuǐ　**120**

WATER shuǐ　水

Ancient form 沝

Catchphrase

WATER from a river often flows around small islands before it enters the sea. **WATER** is 水 shuǐ.

Stroke order

丨 刀 水 水

Radical/Component 目 eye 睡 SLEEP shuì **121**

SLEEP shuì 睡

Ancient form 睡

目 目 (eye) + 垂 垂 (closed) = sleep

Catchphrase

My eyes are drooping and I am falling aSLEEP. SLEEP is 睡 shuì.

Stroke order

| 丨 | 冂 | 冂 | 月 | 目 | 目 | 盱 | 盰 | 盰 | 睡 | 睡 | 睡 | 睡 |

Radical/Component 讠 language 说（說）SPEAK/SAY shuō **122**

SPEAK/SAY shuō 说

Ancient form 說   Traditional form 說

讠 讠 (language) + 兑 兑 (exchange) = speak

Catchphrase

To SPEAK with others is to exchange information with them. SPEAK is 说 shuō.

Stroke order

| 丶 | 讠 | 讠 | 讠 | 讠 | 说 | 说 | 说 | 说 |

Radical/Component 囗 enclosure 四 FOUR sì **123**

FOUR sì 四

Ancient form 四

Catchphrase

Our FOUR-metre high, fortified wall has been defaced with graffiti. FOUR is 四 sì.

Stroke order

| 丨 | 冂 | 四 | 四 | 四 |

| Radical/Component 山 mountain/hill | 岁（歲）AGE suì | 124 |

AGE suì 岁

Traditional form 歲

⛰ (mountain) + ☽ (crescent) = age; year(s) old

Catchphrase

The moon's **AGE** was as great as the mountain's. **AGE** is 岁 suì.

Stroke order

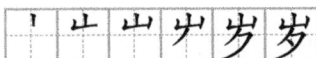

| Radical/Component 亻 human | 他 HE tā | 125 |

HE tā 他

Ancient form 𠤎

亻(human) + 𧎮 (snake) = he/him

Catchphrase

The man runs away expressing that **HE** is afraid of a snake! **HE** is 他 tā.

Stroke order

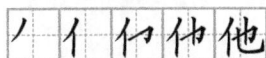

| Radical/Component 女 woman | 她 SHE tā | 126 |

SHE tā 她

女 (woman) + 𧎮 (snake) = she/her

Catchphrase

The woman runs away expressing that **SHE** is afraid of a snake! **SHE** is 她 tā.

Stroke order

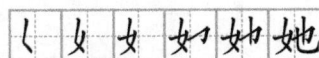

Radical/Component — the first stroke of the character 太 TOO tài | 127

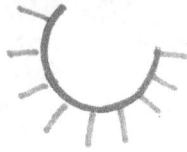

TOO tài 太

Ancient form 太

大（big）+ ▬ (emphasis mark) = too

Catchphrase

If a man jumps TOO high, he risks being burnt by the sun! TOO is 太 tài.

Stroke order

一 ナ 大 太

Radical/Component — sky/heaven 天 SKY tiān | 128

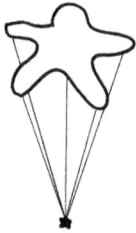

SKY tiān 天

Ancient form 禾

▬ 一 (skyline) + 大 大 (big) = sky

Catchphrase

When we think big, the SKY is the limit! SKY is 天 tiān.

Stroke order

一 二 チ 天

Radical/Component 口 mouth 听（聽）LISTEN tīng | 129

LISTEN tīng 听

Ancient form 𣍘 Traditional form 聽

口 口 (mouth/speak) + 斥 斤 (axe) = listen

Catchphrase

In the presence of malicious speech, Confucius advises us not to LISTEN and instead cut off our ears with a metaphorical axe. LISTEN is 听 tīng.

Stroke order

丨 冂 口 叮 听 听 听

Radical/Component 冂 accommodation　同 TOGETHER tóng　**130**

TOGETHER tóng　同

Ancient form 𠔼

廾 (hand by hand) + 口 (water or resources) = share/together

Catchphrase

Sharing resources and working **TOGETHER** produces the best results. **TOGETHER** is 同 tóng.

Stroke order

Radical/Component 口 mouth　喂 HELLO wèi　**131**

HELLO wèi　喂

Ancient form

口 (mouth) + 畏 (something strange) = hello

Catchphrase

HELLO! It's me calling. HELLO is 喂 wèi!

Stroke order

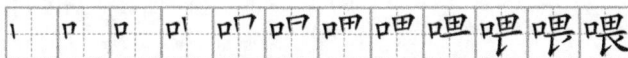

Radical/Component 戈 axe　我 I/ME/SELF wǒ　**132**

I/ME/SELF wǒ　我

Ancient form

手 (arm) + 戈 (axe) = I/me/self

Catchphrase

In ancient history, a man would seldom venture out without a weapon in hand so that he could protect him **SELF** from wild animals. **I/ME/SELF** is 我 wǒ.

Stroke order

Radical/Component — the first stroke of the character 五 FIVE wǔ | 133

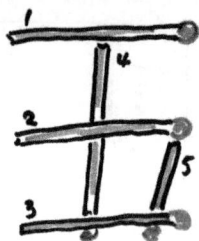

FIVE wǔ 五

Ancient form 𝕏

三（3）＋1＋1＝five

Catchphrase

Number three in Chinese with the addition of the Arabic numerals 1+1, equals FIVE when added together. FIVE is 五 wǔ.

Stroke order

一 丁 五 五

Radical/Component 丿 the first stroke of the character 午 NOON wǔ | 134

NOON wǔ 午

Ancient form ↑

Catchphrase

Beijing is too hot at NOON in the summer. NOON is 午 wǔ.

Stroke order

丿 𠂉 乍 午

Radical/Component 西 west 西 WEST xī | 135

WEST xī 西

Ancient form 𢆶

Catchphrase

Here are two lovely birds staying together to appreciate the sunset in the WEST. WEST is 西 xī.

Stroke order

一 丆 丙 両 西 西

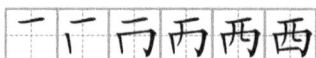

PRACTISE xí 　习

Traditional form 習

Catchphrase
This baby bird has to **PRACTISE** before he can head in the right direction! **PRACTISE** 习 is xí.

Stroke order

丁	刁	习

HAPPY xǐ 　喜

Ancient form 𡔛

𡔛 (pray for producing more children) ＋ ⩊ (sacrificial wine) ＝ joyful; happy

Catchphrase
Celebrate the **HAPPY** marriage with wishes for more children and more food. **HAPPY** is 喜 xǐ.

Stroke order

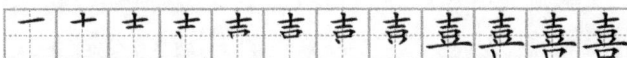

一	十	土	士	吉	吉	吉	吉	壴	壴	喜	喜

SYSTEM xì 　系

Ancient form 𦃽

𠂆 (hand) ＋ 𢇁 (silk cocoons) ＝ tie; system

Catchphrase
Silk threads are often used to **TIE** together hanging lanterns. **TIE/SYSTEM** is 系 xì.

Stroke order

一	二	三	玄	玄	乎	系	系

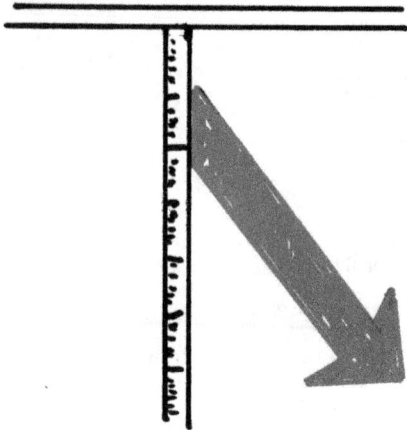

DOWN xià 下

Ancient form 下

Catchphrase
My shares are going DOWN fast. DOWN is 下 xià.

Stroke order

一 丁 下

AHEAD/BEFORE xiān 先

Ancient form 先

屮 (stop pace) + 儿 (people) = ahead/before

Catchphrase
It is the dream of every athlete to reach the finishing line AHEAD of others. AHEAD/BEFORE is 先 xiān.

Stroke order

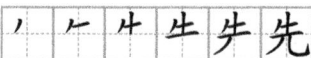

APPEAR xiàn 现

Ancient form 現 Traditional form 現

王 王 (jade) + 貝 见 (seen) = appear/present

Catchphrase
When the mellow beauty of jade first APPEARed before human eyes, it must have been a pleasant surprise! APPEAR/PRESENT is 现 xiàn.

Stroke order

| Radical/Component 心 heart | 想 MISS/THINK xiǎng | 142 |

MISS/THINK xiǎng 想

Ancient form 想

相 相 (picture) + 心 心 (heart) = think/miss

🎧 **Catchphrase**
🗣 When I **MISS** you, I can see you in my mind. **MISS/THINK** is 想 xiǎng.

Stroke order

一 十 十 木 机 机 相 相 相 相 想 想 想

| Radical/Component 小 small/little | 小 LITTLE/SMALL xiǎo | 143 |

LITTLE/SMALL xiǎo 小

Ancient form 小

🎧 **Catchphrase**
🗣 This character looks like a **LITTLE** penguin trying to balance itself with its two wings. **LITTLE/SMALL** is 小 xiǎo.

Stroke order

丨 小 小

| Radical/Component 木 wood/tree | 校 SCHOOL xiào | 144 |

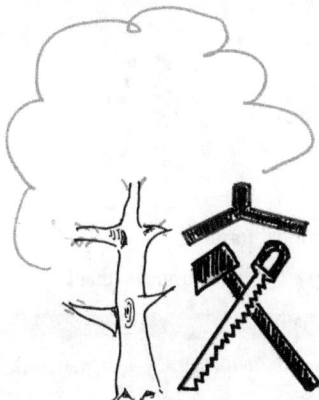

SCHOOL xiào 校

Ancient form 校

木 木 (trees) + 交 交 (connect/communicate) = school

🎧 **Catchphrase**
🗣 For our ancestors, nature was their **SCHOOL**. Communicating with the environment taught them how to survive in the wild. **SCHOOL** is 校 xiào.

Stroke order

一 十 十 木 木 杧 杧 校 校 校

Lesson 13 145—156 些、写、谢、星、兴、学、样、一、衣、医、椅、影

Radical/Component 二 two 些 SOME xiē **145**

SOME xiē 些

Ancient form

止 止 (halt/stop) + 𠤎 匕 (men) + 二 二 (two objects) = few/a few/some; plural measure word

Catchphrase

This cartoon shows two men arguing over SOME matter. SOME is 些 xiē.

Stroke order

丨	卜	屮	止	此	此	此	些	些

Radical/Component 宀 roof 写（寫）WRITE xiě **146**

WRITE xiě 写

Traditional form 寫

宀（roof）+ 与（and/with）= write

Catchphrase

Stay indoors and do some WRITING. WRITE is 写 xiě.

Stroke order

丶	冖	冖	写	写

Radical/Component 讠 language 谢（謝）THANK xiè **147**

THANK xiè 谢

Ancient form　Traditional form 謝

言 讠 (language)+ 身 身 (human body) + 弓 寸 (measure) = thank

Catchphrase

When we say THANK you, we not only use words but also a well-judged bow. THANK is 谢 xiè.

Stroke order

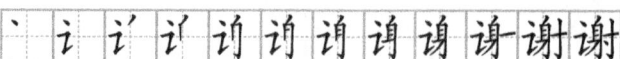

丶	讠	讠	订	诃	诃	诮	诮	谢	谢

Radical/Component 日 sun   星 STAR xīng   **148**

STAR xīng 星

Ancient form

日 (planets) + 生 (grow) = star

Catchphrase

There are countless **STARS** in the sky, but only one is visible through the polluted air. **STAR** is 星 xīng.

Stroke order

Radical/Component 丶 The first stroke of the character   兴（興）EXCITING xìng   **149**

EXCITING xìng 兴

Traditional form 興

Catchphrase

This boy looks like he is enjoying an **EXCITING** moment on his skateboard. **EXCITING** is 兴 xìng.

Stroke order

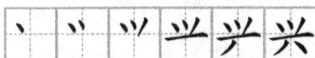

Radical/Component 子 children/man   学（學）STUDY xué   **150**

STUDY xué 学

Traditional form 學

丷 (knowledge) + ∩ 宀 (roof) + 子 (child) = study

Catchphrase

A boy who **STUDIES** hard will one day grasp the three-pronged knowledge of courage, wisdom and compassion. **STUDY** is 学 xué.

Stroke order

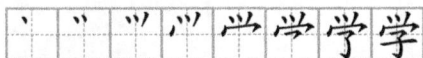

Radical/Component 木 wood　样（樣）APPEARANCE yàng　**151**

**APPEARANCE
yàng**　样

Traditional form 樣

木（wood）+ 羊（sheep）= appearance/shape/sample

Catchphrase

A craftsman shapes a piece of wood into the **APPEARANCE** of a sheep.
APPEARANCE is 样 yàng.

Stroke order

一 十 才 木 术 术 栏 栏 样 样

Radical/Component 一 one　一 ONE yī　**152**

ONE yī　一

Ancient form 一

Catchphrase

Before the beginning of the universe, **ONE** very heavy object existed. **ONE** is 一 yī.

Stroke order

一

Radical/Component 衣 cloth　衣 CLOTHES yī　**153**

CLOTHES yī　衣

Ancient form 衣

Catchphrase

It is best to hang up your **CLOTHES** after use if you don't like ironing! **CLOTHES** is 衣 yī.

Stroke order

丶 一 ㄔ 衤 衤 衣

Radical/Component 矢 arrow　医（醫）MEDICINE yī | 154

MEDICINE yī　医

Ancient form 🏃　Traditional form 醫

⌐ (opened space) + 🏃 (arrow) = cure; treat/doctor; medical science

Catchphrase

In ancient times, practising **MEDICINE** very often involved extracting arrows from wounded soldiers on the battlefield. **MEDICINE** is 医 yī.

Stroke order

一 丁 匚 医 医 医 医

Radical/Component 木 wood　椅 CHAIR yǐ | 155

CHAIR yǐ　椅

Ancient form 檣

木 (tree/wood) + 奇 奇 (rare) = chair

Catchphrase

That **CHAIR** is made of wood and looks strange, but a large person can sit in it. **CHAIR** is 椅 yǐ.

Stroke order

一 十 才 木 杧 杧 栌 柗 梻 梼 椅 椅

Radical/Component 彡 shadows　影 SHADOW yǐng | 156

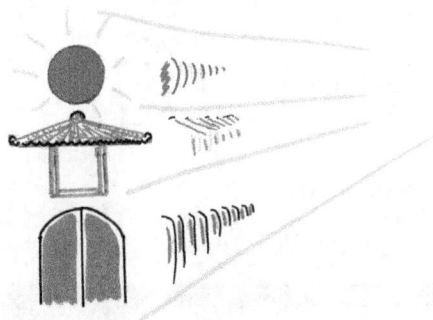

SHADOW yǐng　影

Ancient form 景彡

日 日 (sun) + 京 京 (capital) = 景 景 (landscape of the capital) + 彡 彡 (shadows) = shadow/reflection/trace

Catchphrase

Sunlight falling on a building will create different **SHADOWS** at different hours of the day. **SHADOW** is 影 yǐng.

Stroke order

丶 冂 冂 日 日 日 旦 旱 昃 昙 景 景 景 景 影 影

| Radical/Component 又 hand/again | 友 FRIEND yǒu | **157** |

FRIEND yǒu 友

Ancient form 𢓊

𦥑 (hand) + 𦥑 (hand) = friend

Catchphrase

A good **FRIEND** will always lend a helping hand when it is needed. **FRIEND** is 友 yǒu.

Stroke order

一 ナ 方 友

| Radical/Component 月 organ/moon | 有 HAVE/EXIST yǒu | **158** |

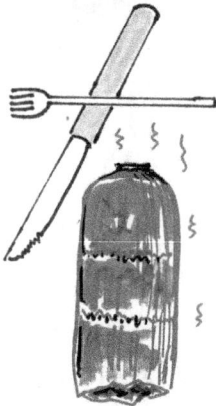

HAVE/EXIST yǒu 有

Ancient form 𠬝

𦘒 (arm and hand) + 𠬝 (organ/meal) = have/exist

Catchphrase

It is lovely to have a hot sausage on a cold day! Do you **HAVE** some at home? **HAVE/EXIST** is 有 yǒu.

Stroke order

一 ナ オ 有 有 有

| Radical/Component 雨 rain | 雨 RAIN yǔ | **159** |

RAIN yǔ 雨

Ancient form 𠕒

— (sky) + 𢆶 (raindrops) = rain

Catchphrase

Water falling from the sky is called **RAIN**. **RAIN** is 雨 yǔ.

Stroke order

一 冂 冂 雨 雨 雨 雨 雨

Radical/Component 讠 language	语（語）LANGUAGE yǔ	**160**

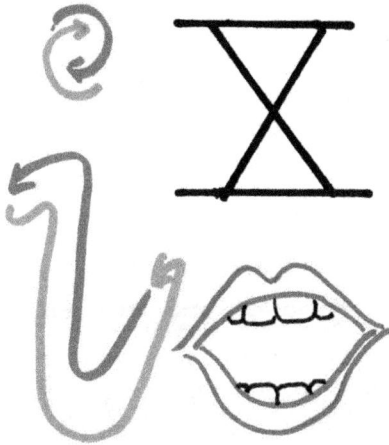

LANGUAGE yǔ 语

Ancient form **🌱**   Traditional form 語

🌱 (language) + 吾 (I/five senses) = language

Catchphrase

If five people talk in different **LANGUAGES** at the same time, they won't understand each other! **LANGUAGE** is 语 yǔ.

Stroke order

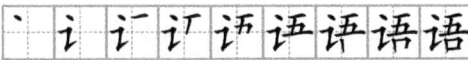

Radical/Component 阝 cliff/steps/wall	院 COURTYARD yuàn	**161**

COURTYARD yuàn 院

Ancient form 院

阝 (cliff /wall) + 完 宀 (roof + 二 married couple + 儿 son=completion/

perfection) = courtyard

Catchphrase

This **COURTYARD** is perfect for a family. It will allow a married couple and their sons to stay together. **COURTYARD** is 院 yuàn.

Stroke order

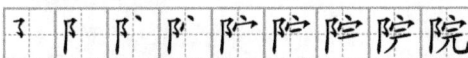

Radical/Component 月 moon/organ	月 MOON/MONTH yuè	**162**

MOON/MONTH yuè 月

Ancient form 🌙

Catchphrase

The brightness of the **MOON** is enhanced by the presence of a light mist. **MOON/MONTH** is 月 yuè.

Stroke order

Radical/Component 一 the first stroke of the character 再 AGAIN zài | **163**

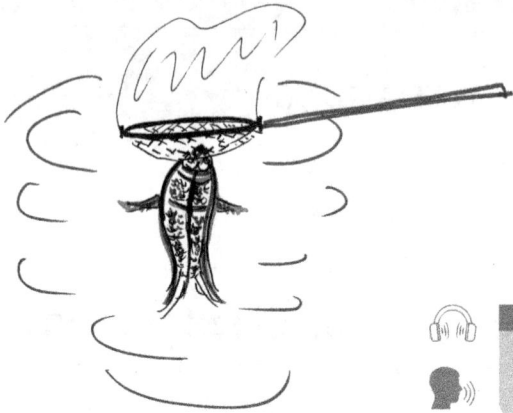

AGAIN zài 再

Ancient form 𦜝

一 (fishnet) + 月 (fish) + 二 (more than once) = again

Catchphrase

If the fisherman throws his net into the sea AGAIN and again, he is sure to catch more than he needs for supper. AGAIN is 再 zài.

Stroke order

一 厂 厃 丙 再 再

Radical/Component 土 land/earth 在 BE LOCATED zài | **164**

IS LOCATED zài 在

Ancient form 㚔

才 (owner's position) + 圡 (land) = be located

Catchphrase

I am the landlord of this piece of land that IS LOCATED beneath my feet. BE LOCATED is 在 zài.

Stroke order

一 ナ 才 在 在 在

Radical/Component 心 heat/mind 怎 HOW/WHAT/WHY zěn | **165**

HOW/WHAT/WHY zěn 怎

乍 (matter) + 心 (heart/mind) = what it is

Catchphrase

This heart is trying to figure out WHAT the matter is. HOW/WHAT/WHY is 怎 zěn.

Stroke order

丿 𠂉 午 乍 乍 乍 怎 怎 怎

Radical/Component 立 stand/erect **站 STAND zhàn** | **166**

STAND zhàn 站

🔺 (stand) + 👣 (occupy) = stand/station

Catchphrase
This wooden sign tells me where I am supposed to **STAND**. **STAND** is 站 zhàn.

Stroke order

丶 亠 ソ 六 立 立 立 立 站 站

Radical/Component 辶 walk **这（這）THIS zhè; zhèi** | **167**

THIS zhè; zhèi 这

Ancient form 🔖 Traditional form 這

辶 (journey/walk) + 👅 (speak/language) = this

Catchphrase
Oh, wonderful, I am finally here. **THIS** is the place I made the long journey for. **THIS** is 这 zhè/zhèi.

Stroke order

丶 亠 亍 文 文 议 这

Radical/Component │ the first stroke of the character **中 CENTRE zhōng** | **168**

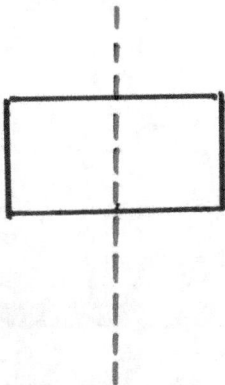

CENTRE zhōng 中

Ancient form ⼗

Catchphrase
A **CENTRE** line divides this rectangle into two equal parts. **CENTRE** is 中 zhōng.

Stroke order

丨 冂 口 中

Radical/Component 金 gold/metal　　钟（鐘）BELL zhōng | 169

BELL zhōng 钟

Traditional form 鐘

金 (gold/metal) + 中 (middle) = bell/clock

Catchphrase

The clapper of a metal BELL is always positioned at its centre. BELL is 钟 zhōng.

Stroke order

丿 𠂉 𠂉 乍 钅 钅 钋 钟 钟

Radical/Component 亻 human　　住 RESIDE/LIVE zhù | 170

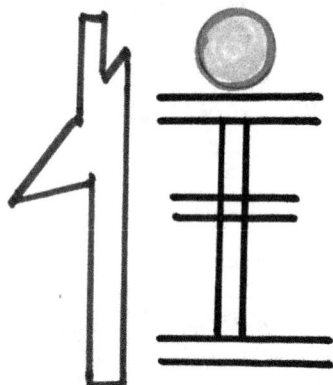

RESIDE/LIVE zhù 住

Ancient form 𨊡

亻 (human) + 主 (main/mainly) = reside/live

Catchphrase

One of the main needs for man is to have somewhere to LIVE. RESIDE/LIVE is 住 zhù.

Stroke order

丿 亻 亻 仁 仲 住 住

Radical/Component 木 tree/wood　　桌 TABLE zhuō | 171

TABLE zhuō 桌

(tall and straight/good) + (wood) = table

Catchphrase

Use good-quality wood when making a tall TABLE. TABLE is 桌 zhuō.

Stroke order

丨 上 上 占 占 卣 皀 卓 桌 桌

Radical/Component 子 son   子 CHILD zǐ; Suffix zi   172

CHILD zǐ; Suffix zi   子

Ancient form 孚

Catchphrase

This figure looks like a **CHILD** learning to move. He is trying to balance himself with outstretched arms. **CHILD** is 子 zǐ, suffix is zi.

Stroke order

⁊ 了 子

Radical/Component 子 son   字 CHARACTER zì   173

CHARACTER zì   字

Ancient form 宇

∩ 宀 (roof) + 孚 子 (son) = character

Catchphrase

A child stays indoors to study **CHARACTER**s. **CHARACTER** is 字 zì.

Stroke order

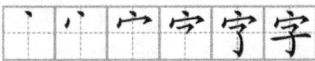
丶 丷 宀 宀 字 字

Radical/Component 禾 crops   租 RENT zū   174

RENT zū   租

Ancient form 組

朿 禾 (crops/harvest) + 且 且 (increase/add)= rent/hire

Catchphrase

RENT used to be paid with grain, and always goes up like a ladder. **RENT** is 租 zū.

Stroke order

丿 二 千 禾 禾 利 和 和 租 租

Radical/Component 日 sun 　昨 YESTERDAY zuó | **175**

YESTERDAY zuó 昨

Ancient form 日止

日 日 (sun) + 止 乍 (carve/just/done/gone/do) = yesterday

Catchphrase

The day which just has gone is YESTERDAY. YESTERDAY is 昨 zuó.

Stroke order

一	冂	冃	日	日'	昨	昨	昨	昨

Radical/Component 亻 human 　作 DO/DONE zuò | **176**

DO/DONE zuò 作

Ancient form 亻止

亻 (human) + 止 (carve/just/done/gone/do) = do/done by a human

Catchphrase

This farmer can now relax, as all his work is DONE. DO/DONE is 作 zuò.

Stroke order

丿	亻	仁	作	竹	作	作

Radical/Component 土 earth/land 　坐 SIT zuò | **177**

SIT zuò 坐

Ancient form 坐

从 从 (two persons) + 土 土 (earth/ground) = sit

Catchphrase

Two people SIT without communicating. SIT is 坐 zuò.

Stroke order

丿	人	丛	从	丛	坐	坐

DO zuò   做

亻 (human) + 故 (ancient) = do

Catchphrase

Before **DO**ing anything, people used to first seek the wisdom of their ancestors. **DO** is 做 zuò.

Stroke order

丿 亻 亻 什 付 估 估 做 做 做 做

词句篇

D | 015 的 Grammatical Code de

Chinese	English	Character codes
我的书	my book	132/015/119
大学的书	university book	015/150/015/119
好的书	good book	039/015/119
我看的书	book I read	132/062/015/119
我昨天看的书……	The book I read yesterday…	132/175/128/062/015/119
我天天看的书……	The book I am reading every day…	132/128/128/062/015/119
我明天看的书……	The book I will read tomorrow…	132/083/128/015/119

DE 的 acts as a suffix. It is placed in between the information words and the noun, so its role is to indicate information that modifies or limits the noun(s). The words indicating information may be other noun(s), adjective(s) or verb(s).

For instance, the phrase in English THE BOOK THAT WAS BOUGHT is BUY DE BOOK (买的书) in Chinese. BUY is a verb and BOOK is a noun. BUY is the information that modifies or limits the book, so it means this particular book was bought from somewhere.

Some word order structures in Chinese are quite similar to English, such as MY BOOK, SCHOOL'S BOOK, YESTERDAY'S BOOK and NICE BOOK. In Chinese these are I DE BOOK, SCHOOL DE BOOK, YESTERDAY DE BOOK and NICE DE BOOK.

In brief, the word that appears before the DE is giving the particularity or detail to the word that follows the DE. The information given can include location, name, feeling or action. The DE is a sign of this construction.

More examples:

1. my book; I DE BOOK

2. his friend; HE DE FRIEND

3. people in the train station; TRAIN STATION DE PEOPLE

4. a store ahead; AHEAD DE STORE

5. a good restaurant; GOOD DE RESTAURANT

6. a pretty woman; PRETTY DE WOMAN

7. a book I bought; I BUY DE BOOK

8. a hospital I went to; I GO DE HOSPITAL

9. a car I drove; I DRIVE DE CAR

L 067 了 Grammatical Code le

Chinese	English	Character codes
我吃中饭了。	I ate lunch.	132/011/168/026/067
我吃了中饭……	I have eaten and finished lunch.	132/011/067/168/026
我天天都吃了中饭去大学。	Every day after lunch has been eaten and finished, I go to the university.	132/128/128/020/011/067/168/026/102/014/150
我明天吃了中饭去大学。	Tomorrow once lunch has been eaten and finished, I will go to the university.	132/083/128/011/067168/026/102/014/150
他做爸爸了。	He has now become a father.	125/178/003/003/067
现在热了。	Now it's getting hotter.	141/164/103/067
我不去北京了。	I won't go to Beijing.	132/007/102/005/059/067
我们不是朋友了。	We are no longer friends.	132/079/007/118/092/157/067

LE 了 and verbs in Chinese

Some of the main differences between English and Chinese have to do with the use of verbs. There are 16 tenses in English, but there appears to be only one in Chinese. In Chinese, the verb form remains the same in different tenses or aspects. This means that Chinese verbs themselves do not necessarily indicate time or state.

To indicate an action that has happened in the past in Chinese, LE can be used.

Let us look at some examples:

1. **LE indicates an action happened in the past.**

    In English: I drank tea.

    In Chinese: I drink LE tea.

2. **LE is also used to indicate an accomplished action or state which will occur in the future.**

    In English: Once tea time has finished tomorrow, I will meet up with you.

    In Chinese: Tomorrow I drink LE tea, and then meet you.

3. **LE can also be used to indicate an accomplished action or state. It indicates not only that the action has been completed but also that the state has ended.**

    In English: I have drunk and finished the tea.

    In Chinese: I drink finish tea LE.

4. **When LE goes to the very last position of a sentence, It indicates a change of the state.**

    For example, someone was previously a teacher but not anymore. The sentence in Chinese is 'He is not teacher LE'. Another example: 'someone has now become a father' is 'he is Dad LE' in Chinese.

5. **TAI...LE Pattern, if the level of an adjective-related topic has gone to an extreme, we would use the TAI...LE pattern. For example, 'the weather is too hot', is 'The weather TAI hot LE in Chinese'.**

在 Grammatical Code zài 163 | Z

at; in; on; locate; stay; exist；ZAI + verb

Chinese	English	Character codes
我朋友在看电视。	My friend is watching TV.	132/092/164/062/ 017/117/089/087
他在做什么?	What is he doing?	125/164/178/111/077/087
他在打电话。	He is making telephone calls.	125/164/013/017/046/087

ZAI 在 usually introduces a location, but it has another important usage which is very similar to -ING in English. In Chinese, however, ZAI is a prefix, not a suffix, to a verb.

Actions that are/were in progress:

English   Chinese

eating   **ZAI** eat

drinking   **ZAI** drink

speaking   **ZAI** speak

N | 087 呢 Grammatical Code ne

Grammatical Code4 087 呢 GRAMMAR "NE"

Chinese	English	Character codes
我在商店，你呢？	I am in the shop. where are you?	132/164/107/018/089/087
我朋友在看电视，你呢？	My friend is watching TV. what are you doing?	132/092/164/062/017/117/089/087
小明在书店买书呢。	Xiaoming is purchasing books in the bookshop.	143/083/164/119/018/075/119/087
他在做什么呢？	What is he doing?	125/164/178/111/077/087
他在打电话呢。	He is making telephone calls.	125/164/013/017/046/087

The use of NE 呢

NE, as an indefinite word, is often used in follow-up questions. For example, 'My father is a teacher, and yours?' In Chinese, this would be 'My father is a teacher. Yours NE?'.To take another example, 'I would love a drink, what about you?' would become 'I would love a drink, you NE?' in Chinese.

The indefinite word NE can be added to the end of a sentence to indicate an action in progress.

English		Chinese
eat	He is eating **at the moment!**	He ZAI eat **NE!**
drink	He is drinking **at the moment!**	He ZAI drink **NE!**
speak	He is speaking **at the moment!**	He ZAI speak **NE!**

吗 Grammatical Code ma 073 | M

Chinese	English	Character codes
你喝茶吗?	Do you drink tea?	089/041/009/073
天气好吗?	Is the weather good?	128/098/039/073
这里是书店吗?	Is this a bookshop?	167/069/118/119/018/073
她是老师吗?	Is she a teacher?	126/118/066/113/073
你在饭馆里吗?	Are you in the restaurant?	089/164/026/035/069/073

Generally speaking, the key or heart of a Chinese sentence always appears at its end, so you can only know its full meaning once the sentence is finished. Therefore, in Chinese, any affirmative sentence can be turned into a question simply by adding the question particle MA 吗 at the end. This is different from English.

A short note on measure words:

When nouns are numbered or pointed to as 'this' or 'that' in Chinese, they carry a measure word related to the class of the noun. For example, chá (tea) carries the measure word bēi (cup). Therefore, zhèi bēi chá means 'this cup of tea'. There are more than 50 special measure words that are commonly used in daily life, but the all-purpose measure word 'ge' (toneless or 4th tone) can serve for most of them.

A | 001 爱 LOVE like/be fond of/take good care of/be in the habit of/be apt to ài

Chinese	English	Character codes
爱 + 人 爱人	love + people lover/partner	001/104
我 + 爱人 我爱人	my spouse	132/001/104
爱 + 国 爱国	love + country be patriotic	001/036
很爱国	be very patriotic	043/001/036
爱家	love + family love one's family	001/053
爱做	love + do love to do	001/178
爱做饭	love to cook food	001/178/026
爱喝	love + drink love to drink	001/041
爱喝茶	love to drink tea	001/041/009
爱漂亮	love + clean + bright love to be pretty	001/093/070
友爱	friend + love love/fraternity	157/001
喜爱	happy + love be fond of	137/001
关爱	care + love concern and care	034/001

> **注释** Note
>
> * 爱人 in terms of social relations only refers to a spouse, like wife or husband.
> ** 和 hé ＝ and

Example Sentences[①]

1/001	Chinese	他爱人是老师。*	
	English	His wife is a teacher.	
2/001	Chinese	爸爸妈妈很关爱我们。	
	English	Daddy and Mummy love and care for us.	
3/001	Chinese	他很喜爱他的狗。	
	English	He is very fond of his dog.	
4/001	Chinese	他爱喝茶和爱吃中国菜。**	
	English	He loves to drink tea and also loves to eat Chinese food.	
5/001	Chinese	A: 大家都去哪儿了？ B: 有一些人在那儿，有一些爱漂亮的人去商店买衣服了。	
	English	A: Where is everyone? B: Some of them are over there; some who love to be pretty have gone to the store to buy clothes.	

---

① 前三句是必学句，相对容易，字体加黑；后两句比较难或长，可以不学，字体不加黑。

Chinese	English	Character codes
八 + 点 八点	eight + point eight o'clock	002/016
八 + 分 八分	eight + minutes eight minutes	002/028
十 + 八 十八	ten + eight eighteen	114/002
八 + 十 八十	eight + ten eighty	002/114

Example Sentences

1/002	Chinese	我们八点去你们学校。
	English	We will go to your school at 8 o'clock.
2/002	Chinese	我今年读了十八本书。*
	English	I have read eighteen books this year.
3/002	Chinese	去北京的火车八点八分开。
	English	The train to Beijing will depart at eight past eight.
4/002	Chinese	他的老师今年四十八岁。
	English	His teacher is 48 years old this year.
5/002	Chinese	他们六个人都是八零后。
	English	These six people were all born in the eighties.

注释 Note

* 本 is a measure word.
Measure words: When nouns are numbered or referred to as
'this' or 'that' in Chinese, they carry a measure word related
to the class of the noun.

B | 003 爸 dad/father bà

Chinese	English	Character codes
爸 + 爸 爸爸	dad+ dad daddy	003/003
他爸爸	his dad	125/003/003
我老爸	my dear daddy	132/066/003

Example Sentences

1/003	Chinese	你爸爸 * 是北京人吗？
	English	Is your father a Beijinger?
2/003	Chinese	他爸爸不是汉语老师。
	English	His father isn't a Chinese teacher.
3/003	Chinese	我爸爸很想我。
	English	My dad misses me very much.
4/003	Chinese	我爸爸有一个很好的电脑。
	English	My father has a very good computer.
5/003	Chinese	爸爸说，他四月不在北京，五月在。
	English	Dad said that he won't be in Beijing in April, but he will be in May.

注释 Note

* 你爸爸 Normally the DE is dropped between pronouns, but in Chinese there is a difference between I DE friend and I friend. The latter is a closer friend than the first. But generally speaking, the above rule applies only when the two elements belong to the same genre. For instance, it is not possible to say I university instead of I DE university.

杯 cup/glass bēi 004 B

Chinese	English	Character codes
杯 + 子 杯子	cup + noun suffix ZI cup/glass	004/172
茶杯	teacup	009/004
一杯水	one cup of water	152/004/120
喝水的杯子	glasses for drinking water	041/120/015/004/172

Example Sentences

1/004	Chinese	这是他的杯子。
	English	This is his glass.
2/004	Chinese	我很喜欢这个杯子。*
	English	I like this cup very much.
3/004	Chinese	这杯茶不好，那杯茶好。**
	English	This tea is not good; that one is good.
4/004	Chinese	这儿的杯子喝水，那儿的杯子喝茶。
	English	The glasses here are for drinking water, and the cups over there are for drinking tea.
5/004	Chinese	妈妈昨天买了四个喝茶的杯子。
	English	Mum bought four teacups yesterday.

注释

*There are more than 50 special measure words in common use for daily life, but the all-purpose measure word ge (toneless or 4th tone) can serve for most of them.

**When nouns are numbered or referred to as 'this' or 'that' in Chinese, they carry a measure word related to the class of the noun. For example, chá (tea) carries the measure word bēi (cup). Therefore, zhèi bēi chá means 'this cup of tea'.

B | 005 北 north běi

Chinese	English	Character codes
北 + 京 北京	north + capital Beijing	005/059
北京 + 人 北京人	Beijing + person people of Beijing	005/059/104
北 + 面 北面	north + side in the northern area	005/081
北站	the North (Railway) Station	005/166

Example Sentences

1/005	Chinese	北京人都 * 爱喝茶。	
	English	The people of Beijing all love to drink tea.	
2/005	Chinese	北面有一个很大的书店。	
	English	There is a very big bookshop on the north side.	
3/005	Chinese	火车北站在哪儿?	
	English	Where is the North Railway Station?	
4/005	Chinese	昨天那个老先生买菜的店不是这个，是北面的那一个。	
	English	This isn't the store where that old man bought vegetables yesterday, (the store where he bought them) is the northern one.	
5/005	Chinese	现在北京的天气和十几年前一样热。	
	English	Nowadays the weather in Beijing is just as hot as a decade ago.	

注释 — Note

* 都 The word dōu, which means 'both' and 'all', is an adverb of scope only and cannot stand by itself. It must always be followed by a verb (or other adverbs).

本 base/origin/notebook/oneself/local/measure word for books běn　006 | B

Chinese	English	Character codes
五 + 本 + 书 五本书	five + measure word（本）+ book five books	133/006/119
书 + 本 书本	books	119/006
本 + 子 本子	notebook	006/172
识字本	recognise + character + notebook primer	116/173/005
本人	origin + person oneself	006/104
本国	origin + country one's own country	006/036
本钱	origin + money capital	006/100
本来	original	006/065

注释　Note

* 谢明先生 In Chinese grammar, Xie's family has a much longer history than the individual Xie has, so the word order should be: family name first, then given name, title.

Example Sentences

1/006	Chinese	谢明先生 * 想买一本书。	
	English	Mr Xie Ming plans to buy a book.	
2/006	Chinese	谢先生买了一本书。	
	English	Mr Xie has bought a book.	
3/006	Chinese	你想不想买几本识字本?	
	English	Do you intend to buy a few primers?	
4/006	Chinese	他的名字在本子上。	
	English	His name is on the notebook.	
5/006	Chinese	他本来是开出租车的，现在上大学了。	
	English	He was a taxi driver and now he is an undergraduate student.	

B | 007 不 no/not bù

Chinese	English	Character codes
不 + 好 不好	no/not + good not good (i.e. bad)	007/039
好 + 不好 好不好?	good + not good Is it good or not good?	039/007/039
不 + 对 不对	not + correct/right not correct/right	007/022
对 + 不对 对不对?	correct + incorrect? Is it correct or not?	022/007/022
不是	not + to be is not	007/118
是不是?	to be + not to be is or isn't…?	118/007/118
不吃	do not + eat don't eat	007/011
吃不吃?	eat + don't eat Eating or not eating?	011/007/011
不热	not hot	007/103
不谢	no need to thank	007/147
对不起	face + no + worth sorry	022/007/097
了不起 *	end + not + worth amazing	067/007/097
不客气	no + polite + air You're welcome.	007/063/098

注释 Note

* 了不起 liǎbùqǐ= amazing

Example Sentences

1/007	Chinese	这家饭馆的菜不好。	
	English	The dishes in this restaurant are not good.	
2/007	Chinese	你认识不认识这个学生?	
	English	Do you know this student or not?	
3/007	Chinese	那个人是不是谢老师?	
	English	Is that person Teacher Xie or not?	
4/007	Chinese	A: 我很冷。你冷不冷? B: 不,我不冷。	
	English	A: I'm very cold, how about you? /Are you cold or not? B: No, I'm not.	
5/007	Chinese	这个医院不是妈妈想去的医院。	
	English	This hospital is not the one Mum wants to go to.	

菜 greens/vegetables/dishes/food cài **008** | **C**

Chinese	English	Character codes
买 + 菜 买菜	buy + greens buy vegetables	075/008
做 + 菜 做菜	make + dishes to cook	178/008
饭菜	food + vegetables food	026/008
热菜	hot + dishes hot food	103/008
北京菜	Beijing food	005/059/008
菜店	green grocer	008/018

Example Sentences

1/008	Chinese	北京菜很好吃。
	English	Beijing alishes are tasty.
2/008	Chinese	来，我们去那家小菜店看看。
	English	Come on, we should go to the small green grocer to have a look.
3/008	Chinese	他会做中国菜，了不起!
	English	He can cook Chinese food. I'm amazed!
4/008	Chinese	昨天中午他做的菜和饭都不太好吃。
	English	The food and dishes he cooked at noon for lunch yesterday were not very good.
5/008	Chinese	A：小明在做什么呢？ * B：他现在坐在椅子上看一本做菜的书呢。
	English	A: What is Xiaoming doing? B: He is sitting on a chair and reading a cookery book.

注释 | Note

    * This 在 + verb + 呢 pattern is similar to 'be + verb + ing' in English and is used to indicate an action is in progress.

C | 009 茶 tea chá

Chinese	English	Character codes
茶 + 杯 茶杯	tea + cup teacup	009/004
中国 + 茶 中国茶	Chinese tea	168/036/009
三杯 + 茶 三杯茶	three cups of tea	106/004/009
热茶	hot tea	103/009

Example Sentences

1/009	Chinese	妈妈在喝中国茶。
	English	Mum is drinking Chinese tea.
2/009	Chinese	这个茶杯很漂亮。
	English	This teacup is quite pretty.
3/009	Chinese	一杯中国茶一块钱。
	English	One cup of Chinese tea costs one yuan.
4/009	Chinese	这儿没有水果，我们买 * 杯茶好不好？
	English	There is no fruit here. Shall we buy a cup of tea?
5/009	Chinese	天冷了，喝杯热茶好吗？
	English	The weather is cold now. Shall we drink a cup of hot tea?

注释 Note

    * In the pattern of verb + number + measure word, if the number is one, it can be omitted.

车 vehicle / bus / coach / train / bike chē 010 | C

Chinese	English	Character codes
租 + 车 租车	hire + car rental car	174/010
出 + 租 + 车 出租车	exit + hire + car taxi	012/174/010
叫 + 出租车 叫出租车	call a taxi	055/012/174/010
火车	train	050/010
电车	tram; trolley bus	017/010
车钱	fare	010/100
上车	get on the vehclde	108/010
下车	get off the vehicle	139/010
在车上	on the train/bus	164/010/108
车站	bus stop	010/166
开车	drive a car/vehicle	061/010
开出租车的人	taxi driver	061/012/174/010/ 015/104

Example Sentences

1/010	Chinese	我天天坐火车去工作。	
	English	I go to work by train every day.	
2/010	Chinese	我没有坐车的钱了，你有吗？	
	English	I don't have the money to buy my bus ticket. Do you have any?	
3/010	Chinese	很多人喜欢在车上看书。	
	English	A lot of people like to read books when they are riding the bus.	
4/010	Chinese	这儿上车下车的人很多，我们去坐电车好吗？	
	English	A lot of people get on and off here. Shall we take the tram instead?	
5/010	Chinese	我们叫的出租车什么时候来？	
	English	What time will the taxi we called arrive?	

C | 011 吃 eat chī

Chinese	English	Character codes
吃 + 饭 吃饭	eat + food have meal	011/026
吃 + 中国 + 饭 吃中国饭	eat + middle + country + food eat Chinese food	011/168/036/026
好 + 吃 好吃	good + eat tasty	039/011
好不好吃？	tasty or not?	039/007/039/011
吃什么？	eat + what what to eat?	011/111/077
吃米饭	eat + rice + food eat cooked rice	011/080/026
小吃	small + eat snack	143/011
做饭吃	make + food + eat make a meal to eat	178/026/011

注释 Note

* 什么 The question word WHAT here is not to form a question. It means WHATEVER or ANYTHING, with emphasis.

Example Sentences

1/011	Chinese	一些有钱人，天天都吃吃喝喝，不想工作。	
	English	Some rich people eat and drink all day long. They don't want to work.	
2/011	Chinese	很多人现在都爱吃中国菜了。	
	English	Nowadays, many people enjoy Chinese food.	
3/011	Chinese	上星期天谢老师做的菜很好吃。	
	English	The meal Mr Xie cooked last Sunday was very tasty.	
4/011	Chinese	昨天我们去的那家饭店的小吃很好。	
	English	The snacks at the restaurant we went to yesterday were very tasty.	
5/011	Chinese	昨天中午，我吃多了，今天什么*都不想吃了。	
	English	I ate too much lunch yesterday, so I won't eat anything today.	

出 go or come out / exceed / exit / turn out / out chū 012 | C

Chinese	English	Character codes
出 + 去 出去	exit + leave go out	012/102
出 + 不 + 去 出不去	out + not + go cannot get out	012/007/102
不 + 出去 不出去	no + exit + leave won't go out	007/012/102
出租	exit + hire rent	012/174
出站	exit + station exit station	012/166
出学校	exit + study + school leave school	012/150/144
出生	out + born be born	012/112
出现	out + appear emerge	012/141
说出	speak out	122/012
看出来	figure out	062/012/065
想出	think out (think up)	142/012
出书	publish	012/119
出名	exit + name be famous	012/082
想出名	want to be famous	142/012/082

Example Sentences

1/012	Chinese	昨天月亮出来的时候很漂亮。	
	English	When the moon came out yesterday, it was very beautiful.	
2/012	Chinese	我 1998 年 12 月 7 号出生在北京。	
	English	I was born in Beijing on 7th December 1998.	
3/012	Chinese	老师站在那儿，我们出不去了。	
	English	We cannot go out anymore because the teacher is standing there.	
4/012	Chinese	她姐姐这三年出了五本书，现在很出名了。	
	English	Her elder sister has published five books in the past three years, so she is now quite famous.	
5/012	Chinese	我看出来了，你不想学习汉语，对不对？	
	English	I can now see that you don't want to study Chinese, is that correct?	

D | 013 打 hit / strike / play / make / fight / take　dǎ

Chinese	English	Character codes
打 + 电 + 话 打电话	make + electronic + talk make a phone call	013/017/046
打 + 人 打人	hit somebody	013/104
打 + 工 打工	take a job	013/032
打字	type	013/173
打听	ask about	013/129
打开	open	013/061
打分	score; mark	013/028
打坐	sit in meditation	013/177

Example Sentences

1/013	Chinese	爸爸妈妈都不能打儿女。	
	English	No fathers or mothers should hit their children.	
2/013	Chinese	他的工作是打电话。	
	English	His job is to make phone calls.	
3/013	Chinese	很多在北京打工的人都不是北京人。	
	English	Many people who work in Beijing aren't Beijingers.	
4/013	Chinese	请大家打开汉语书，我们今天学习二十个汉字。	
	English	Everyone, please open your Chinese textbooks. We are going to learn 20 characters today.	
5/013	Chinese	高先生和大家都不一样，他的家里电视、电脑都没有，有的是一个很好的打字机和一个很老的电话。	
	English	Mr Gao is different from other people. In his home there are no television and computer, instead, he has a very good typewriter and a very old telephone.	

大 big / large / adult / large size dà 014 | D

Chinese	English	Character codes
大 + 人 大人	big + person adult	014/104
大 + 家	big + family everyone	014/053
大 + 学 大学	big + study university	014/150
大学 + 生 大学生	university + pupil undergraduate	014/150/112
大小	size	014/143
大个子	big and tall person	014/031/172
很大	very big	043/014
很大的雨	very heavy rain	043/014/015/160
雨很大	the rain is heavy	160/043/014
大热天	very hot days	014/103/128

Example Sentences

1/014	Chinese	他今年十四岁，不是大人，不能看这个电影。	
	English	He is fourteen years old this year, isn't an adult, and cannot watch this film.	
2/014	Chinese	今天的雨很大，车都不能开了。	
	English	Today's rain is very heavy, so cars cannot be driven.	
3/014	Chinese	北京的热天，人人都睡午觉。	
	English	During the hot days in Beijing, everyone sleeps in the afternoon.	
4/014	Chinese	今天有大大小小二十个人来我们这里吃饭。	
	English	Today we have twenty guests, old and young, all coming to our place for dinner.	
5/014	Chinese	那个大个子是谁？他是哪个大学的（学生）？他叫什么？	
	English	Who is that tall one? Which university does he attend? What's his name?	

D | 015 的 grammartical code de

Chinese	English	Character codes
我 + 的 + 书 我的书	my book	131/015/118
大学 + 的 + 书 大学的书	university's book	014/149/015/118
很好的书	very good book	043/038/015/118
我看的书	the book I read	060/015/118
他买的书	the book he bought	125/075/015/118
我姐姐写的书	the book my elder sister wrote	131/057/057/146/015/118

注释 Note

*Here the character for book at the end has been omitted.

Example Sentences

1/015	Chinese	这个书店的书都是汉语的（书 has omitted word）*。	
	English	All books in this bookshop are in Chinese.	
2/015	Chinese	他喝的茶是不是中国茶？	
	English	Is that tea he is drinking Chinese tea?	
3/015	Chinese	大明的妈妈想买几个好的苹果。	
	English	Daming's mum would like to buy a few good apples.	
4/015	Chinese	我姐姐昨天买的衣服很漂亮。	
	English	The clothes my elder sister bought yesterday are very pretty.	
5/015	Chinese	他爱吃的水果都是中国的。	
	English	All the fruits he loves to eat are from China.	

点 dot / a bit / point / clock time / drop diǎn 016 | D

Chinese	English	Character codes
几 + 点？ 几点？	how many + time What's the time?	052/016
八点 + 二十分 八点二十分	twenty past eight	002/016/025/114/028
茶 + 点 茶点	tea + light refreshment	009/016
一点儿	a bit of	152/016/024
一点儿茶	a bit of tea	152/016/024/009
有（一）点儿*	a bit	158/（152）/016/024
有点儿 + 热 有点儿热	have a bit + hot it is a bit hot	158/016/024/103
热一点儿**	a bit hotter	103/152/016/024
雨点儿	raindrop	160/016/024
多点儿	a bit more	023/016/024
少点儿	a bit less	109/016/024
学点儿	learning a bit of	150/016/024

> **注释 Note**
>
> * 有一点儿热 means a bit hot.
>
> ** 热 一 点 儿 means comparatively hotter than something else.

Example Sentences

1/016	Chinese	A: 今天的飞机几点起飞？ B：今天下午四点二十分起飞。
	English	A: What time will the airplane take off today? B: Today's take-off time is twenty minutes past four.
2/016	Chinese	这杯茶有（一）点儿热，我不喜欢喝热茶。
	English	This tea is a bit (too) hot. I don't like to drink hot tea.
3/016	Chinese	他姐姐会说汉语了，今年想学做（一）点儿中国菜。
	English	His elder sister is already able to speak Chinese; this year she intends to learn a bit of Chinese cooking.
4/016	Chinese	你能不能今天下午四点来？我想先打几个电话。
	English	Can you come at four o'clock this afternoon? I would like to make a few phone calls first.
5/016	Chinese	昨天电视上说，昨天不冷，今天冷一点儿，明天会很冷。
	English	Yesterday on the television, they said it would not be cold, today it would be a bit colder and tomorrow it would be very cold.

D | 017　电 electricity / power / electronic　diàn

Chinese	English	Character codes
电 + 脑 电脑	electronic + brain computer	017/086
电 + 视 电视	electronic + watch television	017/117
电 + 影 电影	electronic + shadow film	017/156
电话	electronic + talk telephone	017/046
有电	have electricity	158/017
没有电	without electricity	078/158/017
电车	electric + vehicle tram	017/010
电能	electric + power	017/088
电热	electric + heat	017/103
电热杯	electric + heat + glass electric cup	017/103/004
电子学	electronic + study electronics	017/172/150
水电站	water + electric + station hydropower station	120/017/166
电钱	charges for electricity	017100
水电钱	charges for water and electricity	120/017/100
电工	electric + job electrician	017/032
电子	electron + suffix	017/172
电学	electric + science electricity	017/150

Example Sentences

1/017	Chinese	前天、昨天都没有电,电脑都不能工作。今天来电了,能工作了。	
	English	There was no electricity the day before yesterday and yesterday, so the computers wouldn't work. Today, power is back, so they could begin to work.	
2/017	Chinese	这几天有一个好电影,叫《没有昨天》,我们一起去看好不好?	
	English	There is a good film called *No Yesterday*. Shall we go to watch it?	
3/017	Chinese	在这个水电站工作的人,有不少是"电大"出来的学生。	
	English	Of the workers at this hydropower station, quite a few graduated from the Open University.	
4/017	Chinese	妈妈说:"现在什么都是电的(东西 -things; here has omitted the things),电钱月月都很高。"	
	English	Mum says, 'Now everything is electronic, so the electricity bill each month is very high.'	
5/017	Chinese	我喜欢电,在大学我学的是电学。我的家里都是"电",电视、电话和电脑。我喝水的杯子是电热的,我去工作都是坐电车。	
	English	I am fond of electricity; I studied electricity at university. At home, everything is electric: the TV, telephone and computer. The cup I drink from is an electric one. I always go to work by tram.	

Chinese	English	Character codes
小 + 店 + 儿 小店儿	small shop	143/018/024
商 + 店 商店	store	107/018
饭 + 店 饭店	restaurant/hotel	026/018
电脑店	computer shop	017/086/018
开店	open a business	061/018
衣服店	clothes shop	153/029/018

Example Sentences

1/018	Chinese	这儿有很多小店，大多都是电脑店。	
	English	There are many small stores here; most of them sell computers.	
2/018	Chinese	这儿有没有一个喝茶的小店？我很想喝一点儿好的中国茶。	
	English	Does this place have a small teahouse? I would really like to drink some good Chinese tea.	
3/018	Chinese	天冷了，我想买大衣了，这儿哪儿有个衣服店？	
	English	The weather is chilly now. I want to buy an overcoat. Where are the clothes shops around here?	
4/018	Chinese	你喜欢的那家商店上午八点开，我们一起坐车去好吗？	
	English	The store you like opens at eight o'clock. Shall we go there together by bus?	
5/018	Chinese	在我们中学的北面，火车站的对面，有一家很好的中国饭店。	
	English	There is a very good Chinese restaurant located in the north of our middle school, opposite the train station.	

D | 019 东 east/ownership dōng

Chinese	English	Character codes
东 + 北 东北	north + east northeast	019/005
东 + 西 东西	east + west things	019/135
东 + 京 东京	east + capital Tokyo	019/059
东站	East Station	019/166
东面	east side	019/081
东家	owner	019/053
做东	play the host	178/019

Example Sentences

1/019	Chinese	我们说了：今天中饭我做东。	
	English	As we agreed, I am going to pay the bill for today's lunch.	
2/019	Chinese	中国的东北和西北都很大。	
	English	China's Northeast and Northwest regions are both very big.	
3/019	Chinese	火车站在那家工人医院的东面。	
	English	The train station is located in the east of the Worker's Hospital.	
4/019	Chinese	你看，东面来的那个人是不是我们的小学老师？	
	English	Look, that person coming from the east is our primary school teacher, right?	
5/019	Chinese	现在很多很好的东西都是中国做的（东西 has ommited），我很高兴！	
	English	I am very happy now that so many very good products are made in China!	

都 both / all / almost dōu 020 | D

Chinese	English	Character codes
都 + 好 都 好	all/both are good	020/039
都 + 不好 都不好	none of them are good	020/007/039
不 + 都好 不都好	not all of them are good	007/020/039
都学	all/both study	020/150
都是	all/both are	020/118
大都是	most of them are	014/020/118

Example Sentences

1/020	Chinese	他们五个人的汉语都很好。	
	English	All five of them have a good command of Chinese.	
2/020	Chinese	这三十本书，没有一本是汉语的。	
	English	Out of these thirty books, none of them are Chinese.	
3/020	Chinese	我的老师和你的老师都不喜欢看老电影。	
	English	Neither my teacher nor your teacher likes to watch old films.	
4/020	Chinese	在北京，那些开出租车的人大都不是北京人。	
	English	In Beijing, most of the people who drive taxis aren't Beijingers.	
5/020	Chinese	我爸爸很爱看书，他什么书都看。	
	English	My dad is very fond of reading books. He reads any book.	

D | 021　读 read / study / read aloud　dú

Chinese	English	Character codes
读 + 书 读书	read aloud + book reading	021/119
会 + 读 + 书 会读书	know how + read + book be good at reading or study	049/021/119
听说读写	listening, speaking, reading and writing	129/122/021/146
想读书	intend + read + book want to be educated	142/021/119
读书人	scholar	021/119/104

Example Sentences

1/021	Chinese	我小时候很爱读书，现在不爱了。
	English	When I was young, I loved reading, but now I don't love reading anymore.
2/021	Chinese	我们的医生是个很会读书的人，他一年能读几十本书。
	English	Our doctor is a very well-read person; he can read dozens of books a year.
3/021	Chinese	谢老师（的）儿子的汉语很好，他的听说读写都好。
	English	Mr Xie's son has a good command of Chinese. He is good at listening, speaking, reading and writing.
4/021	Chinese	学校对面书店里有一个很喜欢读书的人，他不买书，他天天在那里看书。
	English	There is a man in the bookshop opposite our school who likes to read very much. He stays and reads each day, but doesn't buy any books.
5/021	Chinese	我很喜欢一面工作一面读书、学习的人，他们很了不起！
	English	I really like people who study while working, they are great!

对 right/correct/face/to duì 022 | D

Chinese	English	Character codes
不 + 对 不对	not + right/correct not correct	007/022
对 + 不 + 对 对不对？	right + not + right/correct right or not?	022/007/022
很 + 对 很对	right indeed	043/022
说对了	said correctly	122/022/067
对话	dialogue	022/046
一对儿	a pair	152/022/024
对不起	sorry	022/007/097
对面	opposite	022/081
写对了	wrote correctly	146/022/067
你对她说	you speak to her	089/022/126/122

Example Sentences

1/022	Chinese	这个汉字他写对了。	
	English	This Chinese character he wrote is correct.	
2/022	Chinese	那一对儿人在做什么？在买衣服吗？	
	English	What is that couple doing over there? Are they buying clothes?	
3/022	Chinese	对不起，我朋友今天不能来了。	
	English	Sorry, my friend cannot come today.	
4/022	Chinese	对吃苹果，我没有那么喜欢。这个商店有没有中国茶？	
	English	I am not interested in eating apples. Does this store have Chinese tea?	
5/022	Chinese	我很喜欢和中国人对话。	
	English	I like conversing with Chinese people very much.	

D | 023 多 many/a lot/more duō

Chinese	English	Character codes
不 + 多 不多	not + many not many	007/023
多 + 不 + 多 多不多？	many + not many Is it a lot or not?	023/007/023
大 + 多 大多	big + many the most of	014/023
多少？	more + less How many?	023/109
多看	read more	023/062
多看书	read more books	023/062/119
人多	many people	104/023
车很多	so much traffic	010/043/023
不多不少	not more and not less, the right number	007/023/007/109
多热?	How hot is it?	023/103
多子	more children	023/172
多国	many countries	023/036

Example Sentences

1/023	Chinese	你们学校学习汉语的人多不多?
	English	Are there many people studying Chinese at your school?
2/023	Chinese	这些苹果多少钱?
	English	How much do these apples cost?
3/023	Chinese	前面商店里的人多不多?
	English	Are there many people inside the store ahead?
4/023	Chinese	A: 车上的人很多，有没有关系? B: 没关系，我们上去。
	English	A: There are many people on the bus. Is it alright for you? B: It doesn't matter. Let's get on.
5/023	Chinese	他女儿在学汉语，想多看一点儿汉语书。
	English	His daughter is learning Chinese, and he plans to read more Chinese books.

儿 son / child / suffix of certain words ér 024 | E

Chinese	English	Character codes
儿 + 子 儿子	son + noun suffix ZI son	024/172
女 + 儿 女儿	female + child daughter	091/024
明 + 儿 明儿	bright + ER (r-ending retrof lexion) tomorrow	083/024
儿女	son + daughter children	024/091
大儿子	the eldest son	014/024/172
小儿子	the youngest son	143/024/172

Example Sentences

1/024	Chinese	我儿子在这个火车站工作，我女儿在大学读书。	
	English	My son works in this train station; my daughter is an undergraduate student.	
2/024	Chinese	老谢有三个儿子，大儿子工作了，二儿子在上大学，小儿子在上中学。	
	English	Old Xie has three sons, the eldest one has a job now, the second one is a university student, and the youngest one is in middle school.	
3/024	Chinese	老北京说"明天"是"明儿"。"明儿"是老北京话。	
	English	Old Beijingers say 'tomorrow' as minger, which is the Beijing dialect.	
4/024	Chinese	他的儿女我都认识，小的一个名字叫谢明明，大的那个叫谢大明。	
	English	I know both his children. The younger one's name is Xie Mingming and the elder one is called Xie Daming.	
5/024	Chinese	在现在的中国，儿女大了以后，很多都不喜欢和爸爸妈妈住在一起。	
	English	Nowadays in China, after children grow up, most of them don't like to stay with their parents.	

E | 025 二 two èr

Chinese	English	Character codes
二 + 月 二月	two + month February	025/162
二 + 十 二十	two + ten (double ten) twenty	025/114
老 + 二 老二	the second (son or daughter)	066/025
二中	the Number 2 Middle School	066/168
二月二号	the second day of February	025/162/025/040
星期二	Tuesday	148/096/025

Example Sentences

1/025	Chinese	你姐姐是不是十一月二号生的?	
	English	Was your sister born on 2 November (or not)?	
2/025	Chinese	今年的九月二号是星期几?	
	English	What day of the week is 2 September this year?	
3/025	Chinese	我们家的老二在北京二中上学。	
	English	Our second son is studying at Beijing No. 2 Middle School.	
4/025	Chinese	那个东北来的客人星期二中午十二点坐飞机去北京。	
	English	That guest from the Northeast China will go to Beijing at 12 pm on Tuesday by air.	
5/025	Chinese	他很爱吃中国的饭菜，他想一年十二个月、五十二个星期，天天都吃中国饭。	
	English	He is so fond of eating Chinese dishes that he intends to spend the whole year, all twelve months and fifty two weeks, eating Chinese food.	

饭 meal/food/cooked rice fàn 026 | F

Chinese	Englishn	Character codes
饭 + 馆 + 儿 饭馆儿	food + house restaurant	026/035/024
好 + 饭馆儿 好饭馆儿	good restaurant	039/026/035/024
饭 + 菜 饭菜	food and dishes	026/008
饭桌	food + table dinner table	026/171
饭店	restaurant or hotel	026/018
饭钱	food cost	026/100
饭前	before a meal	026/099
饭后	after a meal	026/044
中饭	lunch	168/026
午饭	lunch	134/026
米饭	cooked rice	080/026
做饭	cooking	178/026
做午饭	cook + lunch make lunch	178/134/026
冷饭	cold meal	068/026
热饭	hot meal or reheat food	103/026

Example Sentences

1/026	Chinese	这个饭馆儿有六个饭桌。	
	English	There are six tables in this restaurant.	
2/026	Chinese	中国东北的饭菜和西北的饭菜很不一样。	
	English	The foods in Northeast and Northwest China are very different.	
3/026	Chinese	这儿有饭店吗？我想住四天。	
	English	Are there any hotels here? I'd like to stay for four days.	
4/026	Chinese	我们饭后吃一点儿水果好吗？苹果好不好？	
	English	Shall we eat some fruits after dinner? Would some apples be good or not?	
5/026	Chinese	今天我们有十三个客人吃饭，饭钱是一个人五十九块。	
	English	Today we have thirteen guests for dinner here. The bill is fifty-nine yuan per head.	

F | 027　飞 fly fēi

Chinese	English	Character codes
飞 + 机 飞机	fly + machine airplane	027/051
飞机 + 飞了 飞机飞了。	The flight has departed.	027/051/027/067
先 + 飞 先飞	first destination of the flight	140/027
后飞	second destination of the flight	044/027
不飞了	The flight has been cancelled.	007/027/067
飞起来了	fly + rise + come + LE has taken off	027/097/065/067
坐飞机	fly (as a passenger)	177/027/051
坐上飞机了	sit + above + flight + LE have boarded a flight	177/108/027/051/067
开飞机	pilot an airplane	061/027/051

Example Sentences

1/027	Chinese	昨天我妈妈坐飞机去北京了，她的小狗很不高兴。
	English	My mum went to Beijing by airplane yesterday. Her little dog was not happy.
2/027	Chinese	今天去中国的飞机不飞了，明天上午飞。
	English	Today's flight to China has been cancelled. It will fly tomorrow.
3/027	Chinese	我们不坐飞机，坐火车好吗？我不爱坐飞机。
	English	Let's not fly. Should we take a train instead? I don't like to fly.
4/027	Chinese	你的朋友现在在飞机上了，不能打电话了。
	English	Your friend is now on board an airplane. He cannot call you.
5/027	Chinese	我们的飞机先飞北京，后飞西北。
	English	Our flight goes to Beijing first, and then to the Northwest.

分 minute / divide / penny fēn 028 | F

Chinese	English	Character codes
分 + 开 分开	divide + separate take apart; separate	028/061
五 + 分 + 钱 五分钱	five + penny + money five pennies	133/028/100
二十 + 分 + 钟 二十分钟	20 + minutes + clock 20 minutes	025/114/028/169
分苹果	share apples	028/094/037
十分漂亮	100% + pretty very pretty	114/028/093/070
打分	give + mark give a mark	013/028
分期	divide + period by stages	028/096
分工	division of labour	028/032

Example Sentences

1/028	Chinese	我昨天去北京，坐了四十分钟的火车。	
	English	I went to Beijing yesterday by train. It took forty minutes.	
2/028	Chinese	我一分钱都没有了，你有钱吗？我们买几个苹果吃好吗？	
	English	I don't even have a penny. Do you have some money? Shall we buy a few apples to eat?	
3/028	Chinese	北京火车站十分漂亮。	
	English	The Beijing Railway Station is so beautiful.	
4/028	Chinese	他们分开五年了，现在都有朋友了。	
	English	They have been separated for five years. Now they both already have friends.	
5/028	Chinese	明天请客我和你分工，我去买菜，你做饭好吗?	
	English	Shall we share the work for tomorrow's dinner party. I will buy the food and you cook, OK?	

F | 029 服 dress / serve / obey fú

Chinese	English	Character codes
衣 + 服 衣服	cloth + dress/obey clothes	153/029
校 + 服 校服	school + dress school uniform	144/029
女 + 服 女服	women + dress lady dress	091/029

Example Sentences

1/029	Chinese	妈妈说衣服大了不好看，爸爸说，他喜欢大一点儿的衣服。
	English	Mum says that if clothes are too big, then they do not look nice; Dad says he likes clothes to be a bit bigger.
2/029	Chinese	这个衣服店里的女人衣服都很漂亮。
	English	All the ladies' dresses in the fashion shop are very pretty.
3/029	Chinese	我们女中的校服很好，十分漂亮。
	English	The uniforms of our girls' middle school are very pretty.
4/029	Chinese	那儿的天气很冷，我想多买一些衣服，你看怎么样？
	English	The weather there will be quite cold. I want to buy more clothes. What do you think?
5/029	Chinese	我在北京买的衣服怎么样？好看不好看？
	English	How about the clothes I bought in Beijing? Are they pretty or not?

高 tall/high gāo **030** | G

Chinese	English	Character codes
高 + 兴 高兴	highly + excitement happy; glad; pleased; cheerful	030/149
高 + 大 高大	tall and big	030/014
高 + 中 高中	high + middle school high school	030/168
很高	quite tall	043/030
高分	good mark	030/028
高桌子	tall table	030/171/072
高个子	a tall man/woman	030/031/072

Example Sentences

1/030	Chinese	茶馆儿的桌子和椅子都很高，很好！	
	English	It is good that all the tables and chairs in this tea house are quite high.	
2/030	Chinese	他是一个高个子，这衣服对他有点儿小了。	
	English	He is a tall man. These clothes are a bit small for him.	
3/030	Chinese	这个学期他汉语的分很高，他十分高兴。	
	English	This term he obtained a very high mark in Chinese, and he is very happy.	
4/030	Chinese	他朋友的名字叫高国兴。	
	English	His friend's name is Gao Guoxing.	
5/030	Chinese	我的高中在中国的西北，是一个很好的中学。	
	English	My high school was in Northwest China. It was a good middle school.	

G | 031 个 general measure word/individual gè

Chinese	English	Character codes
五个 + 本子 五个本子	five + GE (measure word) + notebooks five notebooks	133/031/006/172
三个 + 星期 三个星期	Three + GE + star + period three weeks	106/031/148/096
个 + 人 个人	individual person	031/104
一个个	each of everyone	152/031/031
几个/几个?	a few/how many?	052/031
多少个?	how many?	023/109/031
这个	this (one of)	167/031
那个	that (one of)	085/031
哪个?	which (one of)?	084/031

Example Sentences

1/031	Chinese	你去中国几个星期?
	English	How many weeks will you be in China?
2/031	Chinese	这个饭馆儿开了四个月了，他们做的菜很好吃。
	English	This restaurant has been opened for four weeks. The dishes they make taste good.
3/031	Chinese	这儿有三个商店，你说的是哪个?
	English	There are three shops here, which one are you talking about?
4/031	Chinese	他们几个都是我爸爸的学生。
	English	These are all my father's students.
5/031	Chinese	我们有多少个苹果? 有没有三十个?
	English	How many apples do we have? Are there thirty or not?

工 work/job/labour gōng 032 G

Chinese	English	Character codes
工 + 人 工人	work + person worker	032/104
工 + 作 工作	work + do job/work	032/176
工作 + 服 工作服	work + uniform work uniform	032/176/029
工时	work + time working time	032/115
做工	do + work do manual work; work	178/032
小时工	hourly paid job	143/115/032
电工	electricity + work electrician	017/032
开工	start + work start to work	061/032
零工	zero + work casual labourer; odd job	071/032

Example Sentences

1/032	Chinese	他不想天天都工作，他想做零工。	
	English	He doesn't want to do a full-time job. He'd rather do part-time work.	
2/032	Chinese	我的工作服很不好看，我不喜欢。	
	English	My work uniform is ugly. I don't like it.	
3/032	Chinese	我妈妈的衣服很多：工作有工作的衣服，做饭有做饭的衣服，吃饭有吃饭的衣服，睡觉有睡觉的衣服。	
	English	My mum has many clothes: work uniform for working, cooking clothes for cooking, dinner clothes for eating, nightclothes for sleeping.	
4/032	Chinese	现在的工作都是工作多，钱少。	
	English	Today's jobs all consist of lots of work and little money.	
5/032	Chinese	这里的工人大多是西北来的，北京人来的很少。	
	English	The workers here mostly come from the Northwest and people from Beijing are few.	

G | 033 狗 dog gǒu

Chinese	English	Character codes
小 + 狗 小狗	small dog; puppy	143/033
大 + 狗 大狗	big dog	014/033
老 + 狗 老狗	old dog	066/033

Example Sentences

1/033	Chinese	我认识的那个医生很喜欢我们的小狗。	
	English	The doctor I know really likes our puppy.	
2/033	Chinese	狗和猫不是朋友。	
	English	Dogs and cats are not friends with each other.	
3/033	Chinese	漂亮的狗，人人都喜欢。	
	English	Everyone likes beautiful dogs.	
4/033	Chinese	他们家的狗天天下午来我们家睡觉。	
	English	Their family's dog comes to my house every afternoon to sleep.	
5/033	Chinese	我有时候喜欢狗，有时候喜欢猫。	
	English	Sometimes I like dogs; sometimes I like cats.	

关 close / barrier / shut / customs guān 034 | G

Chinese	English	Character codes
关 + 系 关系	barrier + related to relation	034/138
关 + 机 关机	switch off + machine switch off	034/051
开 + 关 开关	on + off switch	061/034
关上	shut + on turn off; close; switch off	034/108
关爱	care of and love	034/001
关电视	close + TV switch off TV	034/017/117
关上电脑	close + on + electronic brain turn off computer	034/108/117/086

Example Sentences

1/034	Chinese	他们在学习汉语，请关上电视好吗？	
	English	Please switch off the TV as they are studying Chinese now.	
2/034	Chinese	这个电脑的开关在哪儿?	
	English	Where is the power switch for this computer?	
3/034	Chinese	这个电视我关不上，你来关好不好？	
	English	Could you switch off this television? I tried, but could not do this.	
4/034	Chinese	高先生和谢老师是朋友，他们的关系很好。	
	English	Mr Gao and Teacher Xie are friends. They have a good and close relationship.	
5/034	Chinese	这个学校的汉语老师对学生们很关爱，学生们都很喜欢他。	
	English	The Chinese teacher of this school cares for his students. All students like him.	

G | 035 馆 a place to accommodate guests/building guǎn

Chinese	English	Character codes
饭 + 馆 + 儿 饭馆儿	food + house + suffix ER restaurant	026/035/024
馆 + 子 馆子	building + suffix ZI restaurant	035/172
茶 + 馆 + 儿 茶馆儿	tea + house + suffix ER teahouse	009/035/024

Example Sentences

1/035	Chinese	这个馆子叫什么名字？
	English	What is the name of this restaurant?
2/035	Chinese	这是一个很好、很有名的茶馆儿。
	English	This is a very good and famous teahouse.
3/035	Chinese	这里的饭馆儿都是中国饭馆儿。
	English	All restaurants here are Chinese restaurants.
4/035	Chinese	我们去那个茶馆儿好吗？那个茶馆儿很小，里面的人很少。
	English	Shall we go to that teahouse? That one is small and has fewer people inside.
5/035	Chinese	北京的茶馆儿很有名，很多人星期六都去那些茶馆儿喝茶和见朋友。
	English	The teahouses of Beijing are famous. A lot of people go to these teahouses to drink tea and meet their friends on Saturdays.

国 country / state / kingdom guó 036 | G

Chinese	English	Character codes
国 + 家 国家	country + family country	036/053
这个 + 国家 这个国家	this country	167/031/036/053
我 + 国 我国	my country	132/036
中 + 国 中国	centre + country China	168/036
中国人	Chinese people	168/036/104
大国	big country	014/036
国很大	the country is big	036/043/014
国不大	the country is not big	036/007/014
小国	small country	143/036
哪国？	which country?	084/036
哪国人？	which country's people?	084/036/104
国学	country + studies classical Chinese studies	036/150

Example Sentences

1/036	Chinese	这个国家的名字叫什么？	
	English	What is the name of this country?	
2/036	Chinese	中国的东北和西北都很大、很漂亮。	
	English	China's Northeast and Northwest are both very big and beautiful.	
3/036	Chinese	中国人大多都说汉语。	
	English	Most Chinese people speak Putonghua.	
4/036	Chinese	有的国家很小，有的国家很大。	
	English	Some countries are very small, some countries are very large.	
5/036	Chinese	北京大学是很有名的国家的大学。	
	English	Peking University is a very famous national university.	

G | 037 果 fruit guǒ

Chinese	English	Character codes
水 + 果 水果	water + fruit fruit	120/037
苹 + 果 苹果	apple	094/037
果 + 子 果子	fruit + noun suffix ZI fruit	037/172
买水果	buy fruit	075/120/037

Example Sentences

1/037	Chinese	那是什么水果？是苹果吗？	
	English	What is this fruit? Is it an apple?	
2/037	Chinese	我妈妈说，好看的苹果好吃，不好看的不好吃。	
	English	My mum says that the apples that look good are delicious and the ugly apples don't taste good.	
3/037	Chinese	这里的水果店很多，我们一起去看看怎么样？	
	English	There are many fruit shops around here. Why don't we go together and have a look?	
4/037	Chinese	昨天我买了一些大苹果，很好吃。	
	English	Yesterday I bought some big apples. They were really tasty.	
5/037	Chinese	我爱吃果子，大果子、小果子都爱吃！	
	English	I love to eat fruits, no matter whether they are big or small!	

汉 Han ethnic group hàn 038 | H

Chinese	English	Character codes
汉 + 人 汉人	Han people	038/104
汉 + 语 汉语	Chinese language	038/159
汉 + 字 汉字	Chinese characters	038/173
老汉	old man	066/038
好汉	brave man; hero	039/038

Example Sentences

1/038	Chinese	这里的学生都很喜欢学习汉字。	
	English	All the students here really love learning Chinese characters.	
2/038	Chinese	这个老汉明天 96 岁，他想请我们去饭馆儿吃饭。	
	English	This old man will be 96 years old tomorrow. He wishes to invite us to a meal in a restaurant.	
3/038	Chinese	高医生写的汉字很漂亮。	
	English	The Chinese characters Doctor Gao wrote were quite beautiful.	
4/038	Chinese	那个好汉是谁?	
	English	Who is that brave man?	
5/038	Chinese	中国西北人说的汉语和中国东北人说的汉语不很一样。	
	English	The Chinese spoken by people in China's Northwest is not the same as that spoken in China's Northeast.	

H | 039 好 good/nice/be fond of/yes/agree hǎo

Chinese	English	Character codes
好 + 人 好人	good man/person	039/104
好 + 不 + 好 好不好?	good or not good?	039/007/039
很 + 好 很好	very nice	043/039
不很好	not very nice	007/043/039
好茶	good tea	039/009
好吃	good to eat; delicious	039/011
好喝	good to drink	039/041
吃好	to eat well	011/039
好吃好喝	to eat and drink well	039/011/039/041
好工作	job is good; a good job	039/032/176
好好学习	study diligently	039/039/150/136
好好想想	think over	039/039/142/142
好大学	good university	039/014/150
好妈妈	good mum	039/074/074

Example Sentences

1/039	Chinese	习医生是一个很好的人。
	English	Doctor Xi is a very good man.
2/039	Chinese	他朋友上了一个好大学。
	English	His friend went to a good university.
3/039	Chinese	这是谁的茶? 这是很好的中国茶!
	English	Whose tea is this? This is very good Chinese tea!
4/039	Chinese	小谢想上一个好大学, 上了大学想有一个好工作, 有了好工作, 想再有一个漂亮的女朋友。
	English	Little Xie hopes to go to a good university. After university, he wants to get a good job. Once he has a good job, he'd like to have a beautiful girlfriend.
5/039	Chinese	妈妈在我去北京的时候对我说： "听妈妈话, 在北京好好学习, 好好吃饭, 好好睡觉。"
	English	My mum said to me when I went to Beijing, ' Take my advice. While you are in Beijing, you should study hard, eat well and sleep well.'

号 trumpet/number/date/size hào 040 H

Chinese	English	Character codes
小 + 号 小号	trumpet/small size	143/040
大 + 号 大号	large size	014/040
电话 + 号 电话号	phone number	017/046/040
今天几号?	What is the date today?	058/128/052/040
三月六号	the sixth day of March	106/162/072/040
住在十六号	live at number 16	170/164/114/072/040
车号	car registration number	010/040
衣服的号	clothes size	153/029/015/040

Example Sentences

1/040	Chinese	昨天是几号?	
	English	What was the date yesterday?	
2/040	Chinese	我现在的衣服大了，我想买小一号的。	
	English	The clothes I'm wearing right now are too big. I'd like to buy one size smaller.	
3/040	Chinese	我家住在十五号，不是二十五号。	
	English	My family lives at Number 15, not Number 25.	
4/040	Chinese	我妈妈昨天买的大衣号不对，大了很多。	
	English	The overcoat my mum bought yesterday was the wrong size. It is much too large.	
5/040	Chinese	我喜欢听小号，我去年在北京买了一个很好的小号。	
	English	I like the sound of trumpets, so I bought a very good trumpet in Beijing last year.	

H | 041 喝 drink hē

Chinese	English	Character codes
喝 + 水 喝水	drink + water drink water	041/120
你 + 喝 + 什么？ 你喝什么？	you + drink + what What do you drink?	089/041/111/077
喝 + 点儿 喝点儿	drink + bit drink a bit	041/016/024
喝多了	drank too much	041/023/067
喝不多	drink + not + many cannot drink a lot	041/007/023
喝热茶	drink + hot + tea	041/103/009

Example Sentences

1/041	Chinese	我不想喝水，我想喝一点儿茶好吗?
	English	I don't want to drink water. I'd like to drink some tea , if that's OK.
2/041	Chinese	那个杯子里是水，不是茶。你想喝茶，我这儿有。
	English	That cup contains water, not tea. If you'd like tea, I have some over here.
3/041	Chinese	妈妈对爸爸说："你能不能多喝一点儿水，少喝一点儿茶？"
	English	Mum says to Dad, 'Can you drink a bit more water and less tea?'
4/041	Chinese	我们明天坐火车去西北，在车上你们想喝什么? 我们一会儿去商店买好吗?
	English	We will take a train to the Northwest tomorrow. On the train, what would you like to drink? Why don't we go to the shop in a moment to purchase it?
5/041	Chinese	我有一个北京来的朋友，他不喜欢工作，他喜欢的是天天和朋友在一起吃吃喝喝。
	English	I have a friend from Beijing who doesn't like to work. Every day he likes to eat and drink with his friends.

和 harmony / peace / and hé 042 | H

Chinese	English	Character codes
我 + 和 + 你 我和你	me and you	132/042/089
和 + 气 和气	harmony + air gentle	042/098
狗 + 和 + 猫 狗和猫	dog and cat	033/042/076
不和	no + harmony conflict	007/042
和好	be reconciled	042/039

Example Sentences

1/042	Chinese	老谢和小谢都是北京人。	
	English	Old Xie and Young Xie are both Beijing people.	
2/042	Chinese	这个商店的衣服和那个商店的衣服我都不喜欢。	
	English	I don't like the clothes in this shop or that shop.	
3/042	Chinese	我的小学和中学都在北京，大学在西北。	
	English	My primary school and secondary school were both in Beijing. My university was in the Northwest.	
4/042	Chinese	我听人说，喜欢猫和狗的人都很和气。	
	English	I was told that people who are fond of dogs and cats are quite gentle.	
5/042	Chinese	坐飞机和坐火车都能去北京，我想坐火车，你呢?	
	English	People can travel to Beijing by plane or train. I'd like to take the train. How about you?	

H 043 很 very / quite hěn

Chinese	English	Character codes
很 + 漂 + 亮 很漂亮	very + clean + bright very pretty/beautiful	043/093/070
很 + 亮 + 吗 很亮吗？	is very bright?	043/070/073
很 + 不 + 很 + 热 很不很热？	very + not + very + hot? Is it very hot?	043/007/043/103
不很热	not very hot	007/043/103

Example Sentences

1/043	Chinese	我们都很好，你们怎么样?	
	English	We are all very well. What about you?	
2/043	Chinese	今天天气很热，昨天不很热。	
	English	Today the weather is very hot. Yesterday it was not very hot.	
3/043	Chinese	对不起，这个电话机很不好看，我不想买。	
	English	Sorry, this telephone set looks really ugly. I don't want to buy it.	
4/043	Chinese	我们前天、昨天和今天都看电影了。前天的不很好，昨天的很好，今天的很不好。	
	English	We watched films the day before yesterday, yesterday and today. The film the day before yesterday was not very good, yesterday's was very good and today's was really bad.	
5/043	Chinese	我们一起去喝茶不很好吗＊？你不高兴吗＊？	
	English	Isn't it very good for us to go and drink tea together? Are you not happy?	

注释 Note

*This is the rhetorical question which one asks for the sake of effect to impress people.

后 later / behind / back / after / last hòu 044 | H

Chinese	English	Character codes
后 + 天 后天	after + day the day after tomorrow	044/128
后 + 面 后面	back + side at the back/behind	044/081
后 + 年 后年	after + year the year after next	044/090
前后	front + back before and after	099/044
后人	later + people later generations	044/104
后果	later + fruit consequences	044/037
后来	later + come afterwards	044/065
后期	later + period later stage	044/096
后妈	stepmother	044/074

Example Sentences

1/044	Chinese	A：谁后天去北京？ B：高小姐后天去北京。	
	English	A: Who will go to Beijing the day after tomorrow? B: Miss Gao will go to Beijing the day after tomorrow.	
2/044	Chinese	我会在明年八月前后去西北大学上学。	
	English	I will go to the Northwest University around August next year.	
3/044	Chinese	火车站的后面是北京医院。	
	English	Behind the train station is Beijing Hospital.	
4/044	Chinese	我姐姐说，她想做一名医生。	
	English	My elder sister said that she would like to be a doctor.	
5/044	Chinese	她很喜欢北京，去年、今年都去了北京，她想明年和后年再去。	
	English	She likes Beijing very much, so she travelled to Beijing last year and this year. She wants to go again next year and the year after next.	

H | 045 候 wait hòu

Chinese	English	Character codes
时 + 候 时候	time + wait time; when	115/045
…… + 的 + 时候 ……的时候	when…	015/115/045
有 + 时候 有时候	have + time sometimes	158/115/045
候车	waiting for a train	045/010
候机	waiting for a flight	045/051

Example Sentences

1/045	Chinese	你姐姐什么时候去北京？
	English	When will your elder sister go to Beijing?
2/045	Chinese	我上大学的时候，有几个说汉语的同学。
	English	When I was at university, there were several fellow students who spoke Chinese.
3/045	Chinese	我有时候喜欢猫，有时候不喜欢。
	English	Sometimes I am fond of cats, sometimes I am not.
4/045	Chinese	我在东北的时候，认识了高小姐，后来，她来了北京，现在我们是同学。
	English	When I was in the Northeast, I met Miss Gao. Later she came to Beijing. Now we are fellow students.
5/045	Chinese	爸爸妈妈都说，吃饭的时候说话不好，有话吃了饭再说。
	English	Dad and Mum both say it's not good to talk during a meal. If you have something to discuss, wait until the meal has finished.

话 speech/words huà 046 | H

Chinese	English	Character codes
说 + 话 说话	speak + words talk	122/046
北京 + 话 北京话	Beijing + words Beijing dialect	005/059/046
话 + 多 话多	words + more talkative	046/023
大话	big + words big talk; boast	014/046
会话	meet + words conversation	049/046
回话	return + words reply; answer	048/046
对话	face + words dialogue	022/046
电话	electric + words telephone	017/046
没话	no + words no words; silent	078/046

Example Sentences

1/046	Chinese	我认识一个老中医，他很喜欢说话。	
	English	I know an aged doctor of traditional Chinese medicine who really likes to talk.	
2/046	Chinese	对不起，我在工作呢，不能回你的电话。	
	English	I am sorry, but I am working now, so I cannot return your phone call.	
3/046	Chinese	我爸爸很不喜欢说大话的人。	
	English	My dad very much dislikes people who boast.	
4/046	Chinese	我昨天在书店的时候，有几个人说北京话，我爱听北京话，北京人说话很好听。	
	English	When I was in a bookshop yesterday, there were some people speaking in the Beijing dialect. I love listening to the Beijing dialect. The sound of Beijing people speaking is very pleasant.	
5/046	Chinese	我在大学学了一年的汉语，我很想和你对话，我们能不能今天下午在电话上对话？你和我都说北京话，好吗？谢谢你！	
	English	I have studied Chinese language for one year at university, so I am quite keen to speak with you. Can we speak on the phone this afternoon? Shall we both speak in the Beijing dialect? Thank you!	

H | 047 欢 welcome/joyful/jubilant/merry huān

Chinese	English	Character codes
喜 + 欢 喜欢	happy + jubilant like	137/047
欢 + 欢 + 喜 + 喜 欢欢喜喜	joyful	047/047/137/137
喜欢 + 吃 喜欢吃	like to eat	137/047/011

Example Sentences

1/047	Chinese	我朋友喜欢吃北京菜。
	English	My friend likes to eat Beijing dishes.
2/047	Chinese	我们都想学和喜欢学汉语。
	English	We all want to learn and like studying Chinese.
3/047	Chinese	你们喜（欢 omittable）不喜欢看这个电影?
	English	Do you like this film or not?
4/047	Chinese	在我的朋友中，有的人喜欢坐飞机，有的人不喜欢，有的人飞机和火车都不喜欢坐。
	English	Of my friends, some people like to travel by plane, some people do not like this and some people don't like to travel by plane or train.
5/047	Chinese	小高这样的人很好，天天都欢欢喜喜，天天都高高兴兴。
	English	People like Young Gao are really good. Every day they enjoy their life and every day they are happy.

回 return / back to / time（measure word）/ reply huí **048** | **H**

Chinese	English	Character codes
回 + 去 回去	return + go return to	048/102
回 + 见 回见	return + meet see again	048/054
回 + 想 回想	return + thinking recall	048/142
回来	return + come come back	048/065
来回	come + back to and fro	065/048
回电	return + electronics call back	048/017
回国	return + country return to home country	048/036
回请	return + invite return hospitality	048/101
三五回	3 + 5 + return several times	106/133/048

Example Sentences

1/048	Chinese	小明，你和你姐姐今年八月回国吗？
	English	Xiaoming, will you and your elder sister return to your home country this August?
2/048	Chinese	我们几个人都想坐火车回去。
	English	A few of us would like to go back by train.
3/048	Chinese	坐飞机去北京来回多少钱？
	English	How much does it cost to travel to and from Beijing by plane?
4/048	Chinese	我的同学请我们吃了三五回了，我们今天一起请他的客好吗？
	English	My fellow student has invited us to eat together several times. Shall we return the hospitality today?

H | 049 会 will / be able to / know how to / meeting huì

Chinese	English	Character codes
会 + 去 会去	will + go will go	049/102
会去 + 北京 会去北京	will go to Beijing	049/102/005/059
会 + 来 会来	will come	049/065
会来 + 吃饭 会来吃饭	will come + eat food will come to eat	049/065/011/026
会说	know how to speak	049/122
会说汉语	can speak Chinese language	049/122/038/160
会做中国菜	can cook Chinese food	049/178/168/036/008
会汉语吗?	to be able to use Chinese language ?	049/038/160/073
开会	hold a meeting	061/049
有会	have meeting	158/049
大会	conference	014/049
会见	meet + see meet up	049/054
会话	conversation	049/046
会客	receive guests	049/063
会面	meet + face meet	049/081

Example Sentences

1/049	Chinese	我和我姐姐后天会去北京大学看我们的汉语老师。
	English	My elder sister and I will go to Peking University to visit our Chinese teacher the day after tomorrow.
2/049	Chinese	高老师说：“不会认和不能写汉字的学生，汉语都不会好。”
	English	Teacher Gao says, 'Students who don't know how to recognize and write Chinese characters will not be good at Chinese. '
3/049	Chinese	我现在去开会，一会儿我们再见面好吗?
	English	I am going to have a meeting now. Shall we meet later?
4/049	Chinese	今天有一些客人来吃饭，他们想吃北京菜，你会做吗?
	English	Today there are some guests coming to dinner. They would like to eat Beijing food. Are you able to cook some?
5/049	Chinese	下午开会，会来很多人，我们看看桌子和椅子少不少。
	English	There are many people coming to the meeting in the afternoon. Let's check if we have enough tables and chairs.

火 fire / angry huǒ 050 | H

Chinese	English	Character codes
火 + 车 火车	fire + engine train	050/010
火 + 气 火气	fire + air temperament	050/098
火 + 热 火热	fire + hot burning hot	050/103
火车上	train + up on the train	050/010/108
上火车	up+ train board a train	108/050/010
火车站	train + station railway station	050/010/166
在火车站里	locate + train + station +inside inside the railway station	164/050/010/166/069
火星	fire + star Mars	050/148
大火	big fire	014/050
起火	catch + fire be on fire	097/050
他火儿了	he + fire + LE (already) he is angry	125/050/024/067

Example Sentences

1/050	Chinese	我住在火车站的北面，米老师住在火车站的西面。	
	English	I live to the north of the train station. Teacher Mi lives to the west of the station.	
2/050	Chinese	火车站里的小吃都很好吃。	
	English	All the snacks at the railway station are delicious.	
3/050	Chinese	天气很冷，饭菜在火上热热再吃好吗？	
	English	As the weather is so cold, should we reheat the food before we eat?	
4/050	Chinese	今天天气火一样热，我们哪儿都不去。	
	English	Today's weather is as hot as fire. We will not go anywhere.	
5/050	Chinese	在昨天的会上，老师说小谢的学习不很好，小谢火儿了。他这个人很不喜欢人家说他不好。	
	English	Yesterday at the meeting, the teacher said Little Xie should have done better in his study and Xie got angry. He is the type of person who really dislikes others saying negative things about him.	

J | 051 机 machine jī

Chinese	English	Character codes
飞 + 机 飞机	fly + machine airplane	027/051
上 + 飞机 上飞机	boarding (a flight)	108/027/051
机 + 上 机上	on board	051/108
电机	electronic + machine electric machinery	017/051
开机	switch on	061/051
关机	switch off	034/051
机会	chance + meet chance; opportunity	051/049
打火机	hit + fire + machine lighter	013/050/051

Example Sentences

1/051	Chinese	很多人喜欢在飞机上看电影。	
	English	Many people like to watch films when they are on a plane.	
2/051	Chinese	人们都说：学习好，工作机会多；学习不好，工作机会少。	
	English	People all say: if you study well, you will have many opportunities in your career; if you do not study well, you will have few opportunities.	
3/051	Chinese	A: 你们星期三下午几点上飞机？ B: 我们四点上飞机。	
	English	A: What time on Wednesday afternoon will you board the plane? B: We will board at 4 o'clock.	
4/051	Chinese	现在开会了，请大家关机。	
	English	The meeting is starting now. Would everyone please turn off their mobile phones.	
5/051	Chinese	我去东北喜欢坐火车，去西北喜欢坐飞机。	
	English	When I go to the Northeast, I like to travel by train; when I go to the Northwest, I like to travel by plane.	

几 how many / few jǐ 052 J

Chineses	English	Character codes
几 + 个 + 人? 几个人?	how many + Measure Word + people how many people?	052/031/104
几 + 个 + 人 几个人	a few + Measure Word + people a few people	052/031/104
十 + 几 + 个 + 人 十几个人	Ten + a few + Measure Word + people between ten and twenty people	114/052/031/104
几十个人	a few + ten + MW + people dozens of people (e.g. 20; 30; 40 etc)	052/114/031/104
没有几个人	do not + a few people not many people	078/158/052/031/104
几分 ?	how many + penny how many pennies?	052/028
几时?	when; what time?	052/115
几点?	what is the time?	052/016
几块钱?	how many+ MW +money How much (money)?	052/064/100
五块几	more than five and less than six yuan	133/064/052

Example Sentences

1/052	Chinese	现在几点几分?	
	English	What time is it now?	
2/052	Chinese	今天来喝茶的人没有几个。	
	English	Today there were only a few people who came to drink tea.	
3/052	Chinese	我昨天买的衣服五十六块零五分。	
	English	The clothes I bought yesterday cost 56 *yuan* and five *fen*.	
4/052	Chinese	A：我们几个人想叫出租车去看电影，你们几个呢？ B: 我们没有钱。这样好吗，你们出钱，我们坐车。	
	English	A: The (small) group of us would like to call a taxi to go to watch a film. How about you? B: We don't have the money. How about this: you pay and give us a free ride.	
5/052	Chinese	我十几年没有去北京了，我很想我在大学时候的同学，很想见见他们。	
	English	I have not visited Beijing for more than 10 years. I really miss my fellow students from university and would really like to see them.	

J | 053 家 home/family/measure word jiā

Chinese	English	Character codes
家 + 里 家里	home/family + inside in the home/family	053/069
家 + 在 家在	home/family + locate home/family is in…	053/164
家 + 人 家人	home/family + people family member	053/104
商家	commercial + home/family business owner	107/053
大家	everyone	014/053
国家	state + home/family country	036/053
作家	write + specialist writer	176/053
汉学家	Sinology+ specialist sinologist	038/150/053
家书	home/family + book family letters	053/119
回家	return + home/family go back home	048/053
家家	every household	053/053
老人家	old + person + home old man	066/104/053
女人家	female + person + home woman	091/104/053
人家	person + home other persons/people	104/053
客家	guest +home/family Hakka people (who originally migrated from the North to SE China)	063/053

Example Sentences

1/053	Chinese	我一个人在东北，我的家人都在西北。
	English	I am alone in the Northeast. My family are all in the Northwest.
2/053	Chinese	A: 你家里都有什么人? B: 我家里有爸爸妈妈和一个姐姐。
	English	A: Who are the people in your family? B: In my family, I have my father, mother and one elder sister.
3/053	Chinese	现在中国人家家都有电视和电话。
	English	Today in China, every family has a television and telephone.
4/053	Chinese	我家住在北京的北面，那里有很多家电脑的商店。
	English	My family lives in northern Beijing. There are many computer shops in that area.
5/053	Chinese	我的汉语老师说："国家是国和家，没有国怎么会有家?"我说："老师，不对。我看，先有家，后有国。没有家怎么会有国呢?"
	English	My Chinese teacher said, 'The word state (in Chinese) consists of two words — country and family. Without a country, how can you have a family?' I said, 'Teacher, that is not correct. In my opinion, first you have a family and then you have a country. Without family, how can you have a country?'

见 see / meet jiàn **054** | **J**

Chinese	English	Character codes
见 + 识 见识	see + knowledge enrich experience/knowledge	054/116
见 + 面 见面	see + face meet someone	054/081
见 + 好 见好	see + good get better/recover	054/039
见习	see + practise be on probation	054/136
会见	meet + see to meet	049/054
看见	look + see see	062/054
听见	hear + see hear	129/054

Example Sentences

1/054	Chinese	我昨天看见老谢在商店买东西，他买了很多吃的东西。	
	English	Yesterday I saw Old Xie purchasing things in the shop. He bought a lot of things to eat.	
2/054	Chinese	这个老师很有见识，他的学生都很喜欢他。	
	English	This teacher is quite knowledgeable. His students are all fond of him.	
3/054	Chinese	我们星期二中午先见面，见了面再去吃午饭，怎么样？	
	English	How about meeting on Tuesday at noon first, then we go to eat lunch?	
4/054	Chinese	小明说，现在下雨了，不想来我家和我见面了。她说，明天天气好了，她再来和我见面。	
	English	Little ming said that it was raining, so she does not want to come to my home to meet up. She said if the weather is good tomorrow, then she will come and meet me.	
5/054	Chinese	我很想认识你的医生，我能下星期和他见见面吗？	
	English	I wish to get acquainted with your doctor. Can I meet him next week, please?	

J | 055 叫 shout/call/yell jiào

Chinese	English	Character codes
叫 + 什么 叫什么？	call + what What is the name?	055/111/077
叫 + 人 叫人	call + people call people	055/104
大 + 叫 大叫	big + call shout	014/055
叫菜	call + dishes order dishes	055/008
叫谁？	call + who call whom	055/110
狗叫	dog's bark	033/055

Example Sentences

1/055	Chinese	A: 你听见狗叫了吗？ B: 没有，我没听见，我们这里没有狗。	
	English	A: Did you hear those dogs barking? B: No, I didn't. There are no dogs here.	
2/055	Chinese	A: 你叫什么名字？ B: 我叫冷小朋。你呢？	
	English	A: What's your name? B: My name is Leng Xiaopeng. What's yours?	
3/055	Chinese	你现在先睡觉，睡一个小时我再叫你，好吗？	
	English	Go to sleep now. I will wake you up in one hour. Is that OK?	
4/055	Chinese	今天吃中国饭我请客。小明，你是北京人，你叫菜好吗？我们都不会点中国菜。	
	English	I would like to invite you to eat Chinese food today. Little ming, you are from Beijing, so will you order the food? None of us know how to order Chinese food.	
5/055	Chinese	爸爸问妈妈："七点了，叫不叫女儿？" 妈妈说："现在不叫，学校九点上课，我们七点四十五分再叫她好不好？"	
	English	Dad asks Mum, 'It is 7 o'clock now. Should we wake our daughter up?' Mum says, 'Not now. School starts at 9 o'clock, so let's wake her up at 7:45, how about that?'	

觉 sleep jiào; sense/feel jué 056 | J

Chinese	English	Character codes
睡 + 觉 睡觉	close eyes + sleep sleep	121/056
大 + 觉 大觉	big + sleep a sound sleep	014/056
小 + 觉 小觉	small + sleep take a nap	143/056
视觉 *	sight	117/056
听觉 *	hearing	129/056
午觉	noon + sleep an afternoon nap	134/056
睡好觉了吗?	sleep + sound + sense + LE + question code Did you sleep well?	121/039/056/067/073
（睡）觉没睡好?	sleep + no + sleep + well sleepless Did you sleep well?	121/056/078/121/039

注释

Note

* 觉 jué=sense; fell

Example Sentences

1/056	Chinese	我在飞机上睡了一大觉，现在不想睡了。	
	English	I slept soundly on the flight, so I don't want to sleep now.	
2/056	Chinese	天气热的时候，很多北京人都睡午觉。	
	English	When the weather is hot, a lot of Beijing people take afternoon naps.	
3/056	Chinese	我昨天没睡好觉，今天想好好睡一觉。	
	English	I didn't sleep well yesterday, so today I want to get a good sleep.	
4/056	Chinese	昨天我坐了一天火车，回了家，我大睡了一觉。	
	English	Yesterday I spent a whole day sitting on a train. After I got home, I slept soundly.	
5/056	Chinese	A: 看你今天的样子很不好，你怎么了？ B: 我昨天没睡好，一会儿中午的时候，我想睡一个午觉。	
	English	A: You look terrible today. What happened? B: I didn't sleep well yesterday. In the afternoon, I'd like to take a nap for a while.	

J | 057 姐 older sister jiě

Chinese	English	Character codes
姐 + 姐 姐姐	elder sister	057/057
大 + 姐 大姐	eldest sister/elder sister (a term of address for a woman oldler than the speaker)	014/057
小 + 姐 小姐	Miss	143/057

Example Sentences

1/057	Chinese	小姐，这里有没有中国茶?
	English	Miss, is there any Chinese tea here?
2/057	Chinese	我朋友的大姐姐是医生。
	English	My friend's eldest sister is a doctor.
3/057	Chinese	他有三个姐姐，大姐、二姐在北京，小姐姐在东北。
	English	He has three sisters. His eldest sister and second sister are in Beijing. The youngest sister is in the Northeast.
4/057	Chinese	大姐，火车站里有中国饭馆吗?
	English	Hi, elder sister, is there a Chinese restaurant in the railway station?
5/057	Chinese	我那个住在北京的大姐去年生了一个很漂亮的女儿。
	English	My eldest sister, who lives in Beijing, gave birth to a beautiful daughter last year.

今 present / now / today / the present / modern jīn 058 | J

Chinese	English	Character codes
今 + 天 今天	present + day today; this day	058/128
今 + 年 今年	present + year this year	058/090
今 + 后 今后	present + later from now on	058/044
今生	present + life this life	058/112
现今	now + present nowadays	141/058

Example Sentences

1/058	Chinese	今天是几号?	
	English	What is the date today?	
2/058	Chinese	昨天是二零一八年，今天是二零一九年。	
	English	Yesterday was 2018. Today is 2019.	
3/058	Chinese	你今后的工作是什么?	
	English	What is your job from now on?	
4/058	Chinese	现今的北京，看电影的人少了，大家都喜欢看电视了。	
	English	In today's Beijing, fewer people watch movies than before. Everyone likes to watch television now.	
5/058	Chinese	我和我爸爸妈妈说了，现今我是老师了，不能天天都去看他们了。	
	English	I have discussed the following with my father and mother: as I am from now on a teacher, I will no longer be able to visit them every day.	

J | 059 京 Beijing / capital jīng

Chinese	English	Character codes
京 + 菜 京菜	Beijing + dish/food Beijing food	059/008
北 + 京 北京	northern + capital Beijing	005/059
北京 + 话 北京话	Beijing + dialect Beijing dialect	005/059/046
老北京	old + Beijing the old generation of Beijingers	066/005/059
北京站	Beijing Railway Station	005/059/166
北京西站	Beijing West Railway Station	005/059/135/166

Example Sentences

1/059	Chinese	我很喜欢吃京菜，你呢？
	English	I really love to eat Beijing food. How about you?
2/059	Chinese	我去北京西站坐火车。
	English	I will go to the Beijing West Railway Station to take a train.
3/059	Chinese	我妈妈是老北京，我爸爸不是。
	English	My mum is an old Beijinger. My dad is not.
4/059	Chinese	北京菜和东北菜很不一样，今天我们去一家京菜馆怎么样？
	English	Beijing dishes are quite different from the food in the Northeast. Shall we go to a Beijing restaurant today?
5/059	Chinese	A: 喂，小姐，北京火车站在哪儿？ B: 在那家书店的对面。
	English	A: Hi, young lady, where is the Beijing Railway Station? B: It is located opposite that bookshop.

Chinese	English	Character codes
九 + 年 九年	nine + year nine years	060/090
九 + 个 + 月 九个月	nine + GE + moon nine months	060/031/162
九 + 十 + 九 九十九	nine + ten + nine ninety-nine	060/114/060
1999 年	one + nine + nine + nine + year the year 1999	152/060/060/060/090
电话 199	telephone number 199	017/046/152/060/060

Example Sentences

1/060	Chinese	谢医生今年九十九岁。	
	English	Doctor Xie is 99 years old this year.	
2/060	Chinese	你是不是九月九号上午九点的飞机?	
	English	Does your flight take off at 9 o'clock in the morning on the 9th of September?	
3/060	Chinese	小明生的那一天是三月十九号，和我一样。	
	English	That date of Little Ming's birthday is the 19th of March, which is the same day I was born.	
4/060	Chinese	我在北京住了九年，在东北住了九个月。	
	English	I have lived in Beijing for nine years and I have lived in the Northeast for nine months.	
5/060	Chinese	高先生的女朋友和他好了九年，现在不好了。他女朋友去北京了。	
	English	Mr Gao and his girlfriend were in love for nine years, but now their relations are bad. His girlfriend has gone to Beijing.	

K | 061   开 open / switch on / start / drive / hold / boil kāi

Chinese	English	Character codes
开 + 会 开会	hold + meet hold a meeting	061/049
开 + 车 开车	drive + vehicle drive a car	061/010
开 + 学 开学	begin + school school term begins	061/150
开饭	start + food food is ready to eat	061/026
开火	open + fire open fire (in a battle)	061/050
开水	boiled + water boiled water	061/120
开关	switch on + switch off switch	061/119
打开书	turn + open + book open the book	013/061/119
水开了	water + open + LE the water is boiling	120/061/067
开电脑	turn on + electronic + brain switch on computer	061/017/086
电视的开关	electronic + vision + DE + switch on + switch off TV switch	017/117/015/061/034
开机	switch on + machine turn on (mobile phone or laptop)	061/051
车开来了	vehicle + drive + come + LE the car is coming	010/061/065/067

Example Sentences

1/061	Chinese	电视的开关在哪儿？
	English	Where is the power switch for the television?
2/061	Chinese	水开了吗？我想喝一点儿开水。
	English	Is the water boiling? I'd like to drink some hot water.
3/061	Chinese	请你们打开书。
	English	Please open your book!
4/061	Chinese	今天是星期六，学校不开饭，我们开车去我们昨天去的北京菜馆好不好？
	English	Today is Saturday, the school dining hall will not be serving food. Shall we drive to the Beijing restaurant we went to yesterday?
5/061	Chinese	小谢，我天天都是上午十点关机学汉语，十二点开机，你下午再打来好吗？
	English	Little Xie, every day I switch off my phone at 10 a.m. in order to study Chinese. I turn it on again at noon, so can you please call me again in the afternoon?

看 watch / look / visit / read / check / opinion kàn 062 | K

Chinese	English	Character codes
看 + 看 看看	look + look to look around/have a look	062/062
看 + 书 看书	read + book reading	062/119
看 + 三 + 本 + 书 看三本书	read + three + MW + book read three books	062/106/006/119
看电视	watch + TV watch TV	062/017//117
看电影	watch + electronic + shadows watch a movie	062/017/156
看不起	look + not + rise look down on/undermine	062/007/097
看上他了	opinion on him LE to take a fancy to him/be fond of him	062/108/125/067
看上去	look + up + a way look like/seem/it looks as if	062/108/102
看见	watch + see see	062/054
看出	check + out make out	062/012
看中	opinion + on fancy	062/168
想看	plan + look want to see	142/062
会看人	know how to + look + people be good at judging people	049/062/104

Example Sentences

1/062	Chinese	谁来了？我出去看看！
	English	Who is coming? Go out and have a look!
2/062	Chinese	钱医生的姐姐来医院的时候，我看见她了，她很漂亮！
	English	When Doctor Qian's elder sister came to the hospital, I saw her. She is very beautiful!
3/062	Chinese	同学们说好了，他们上午去书店买书，下午去看中国电影。
	English	All of our fellow students have agreed they will go to the bookshop to purchase books in the morning. In the afternoon, they will go and watch a Chinese film.
4/062	Chinese	我女朋友说，她昨天在衣服店看中的衣服今天没有了，她很生气。
	English	My girlfriend told me the clothes she liked in the shop yesterday are now gone, so she is really disappointed.
5/062	Chinese	我的一个在东北的同学今年上大学，他看不上东北的学校，想来北京读北京大学。
	English	One of my fellow students from the Northeast is going to university this year. He looks down on colleges in the Northeast and wants to come to Beijing and to be admitted to Peking University.

K | 063 客 polite/guest/visitor/customer kè

Chinese	English	Character codes
客 + 人 客人	polite+person guest/customer	063/104
客 + 车 客车	passenger + car/train bus	063/010
大客车	coach	014/063/010
客店	guest + business house hotel	063/018
客饭	guest + food set meal	063/026
客机	guest + plane airliner	063/051
客家人	guest + home + people Hakka people	063/053/104
客商	guest + trade travelling trader	063/107
请客	invite + guest treat sb. a meal	101/063
来客	come + guest guest	065/063

Example Sentences

1/063	Chinese	今天有两个客商来。
	English	Two businessmen will come today.
2/063	Chinese	下个星期一大姐 28 岁，我们一块儿去吃中国饭好不好？我请客。
	English	Our eldest sister will be 28 years old next Monday. Can we eat Chinese food to celebrate? I will pay the bill.
3/063	Chinese	妈妈明天下午坐大客车来。
	English	Mum will arrive here by coach tomorrow afternoon.
4/063	Chinese	书店的人对客人都很客气。
	English	All the staff in the bookshop are polite to their customers.
5/063	Chinese	这个学校很好，老师对学生都很客气。
	English	This school is very good. The teachers are all very polite.

块 piece/MW for currency kuài 064 | K

Chinese	English	Character codes
一 + 块 + 钱 一块钱	one yuan	152/064/100
三 + 十 + 五 + 块 三十五块	35 yuan	106/114/133/064
五 + 十 + 五 + 块 + 五 五十五块五	55 yuan and 50 fen	133/114/133/064/133
几块钱?	how much	052/064/100
一块吃的东西	one piece of an edible thing	152/064/011/015/019/135

Example Sentences

1/064	Chinese	这三小块苹果你吃不吃?
	English	Would you like to eat these three small pieces of apple?
2/064	Chinese	你有两块钱吗?
	English	Do you have two yuan?
3/064	Chinese	这本书三十块钱。
	English	This book costs 30 yuan.
4/064	Chinese	A：这五个苹果是一块五吗? B：是。 A：好，我买。
	English	A: Do these five apples cost one yuan fifty? B: Yes, that's right. A: Good, I will buy them.
5/064	Chinese	A：这杯热茶三块零五分。 B：这是四块。 A：你有零钱吗? B：我没有。 A：好，三块。
	English	A: This cup of hot tea is three yuan and five fen. B: Here are four yuan. A: Do you have some small change? B: I don't. A: Alright, I'll make it three yuan.

L | 065 来 come/coming/receive/order lái

Chinese	English	Character codes
来 + 年 来年	come + year the coming year	065/090
来 + 回 来回	return	065/048
来 + 来 + 回 + 回 来来回回	over and over again	065/065/048/048
回来	come back	048/065
会来	will come	049/065
想来	would like to come	142/065
不回来了	will not return	007/048/065/067
三天没回来	did not come back for three days	106/128/078/048/065/
三天不回来	will not return for three days	106/128/007/048/065
来来去去	coming and going	065/065/102/102

Example Sentences

1/065	Chinese	妈妈明天回来，我们都很高兴。
	English	My mum will come back tomorrow. We are all very happy.
2/065	Chinese	钱医生去北京了，不回来了。
	English	Doctor Qian has gone back to Beijing and will not return.
3/065	Chinese	天下雨了，很冷，猫怎么没回来？
	English	The weather is rainy and it's very cold. Why hasn't the cat come back?
4/065	Chinese	小谢来北京十天都没回家，他爸爸很生气。
	English	Little Xie has been in Beijing for ten days and still hasn't come home. His father is very angry.
5/065	Chinese	小谢昨天对我说："我想去你家学汉语，你妈妈会不会不高兴？"我说："我妈妈很喜欢朋友来我家，她不会不高兴。"
	English	Little Xie said to me yesterday, 'I would like to go to your home to study Chinese. Will your mother be unhappy?' I said, 'My mum really likes friends visiting our home, so she would not be unhappy.'

老 old/elder/experienced/senior/always lǎo 066 | L

Chinese	English	Character codes
老 + 师 老师	old+master teacher	066/113
老 + 汉 老汉	old+man old man	066/038
老 + 人 老人	old + person elderly	066/104
老店	old shop	066/018
老家	old+home hometown	066/053
老了	old + grammar code getting old	066/067
老来	old + come always come	066/065
老朋友	old friend	066/092/157
老客人	old customer	066/063/104
老车	old car	066/010
老电影	old + electricity + shadow old movie	066/017/156
老话	old + speech old saying	066/046
老大	the eldest	066/014
老年	the aged	066/090
老天	Heaven	066/128
很老	very old	043/066
太老了	too old*	127/066/067
老太太 **	old woman	066/127/127
老老小小	old and young	066/066/143/143

注释 Note

* The TAI...LE pattern.
** 太太 tàitai=Mrs; madame

Example Sentences

1/066	Chinese	看，他们一家老老小小都来了！	
	English	Look, their whole family, old and young, have arrived.	
2/066	Chinese	谢小姐是谢家的老大。	
	English	Miss Xie is the eldest child in her family.	
3/066	Chinese	我（的）爸爸妈妈都很喜欢看老电影。	
	English	My dad and mum both love to watch old films.	
4/066	Chinese	这家衣服店是很老的店了，店里来的人都是老客人、老朋友。	
	English	This clothes shop is very old. The people who come here are either old customers or old friends.	
5/066	Chinese	我的老家在东北，小时候天天都说东北话。	
	English	My hometown is in the Northeast. When I was young, I always spoke in a northeastern dialect.	

L | 067 了 grammatical code le

Chinese	English	Character codes
去 + 北京 + 了 去北京了	go+north+capital+LE went to Beijing	102/005/059/067
去 + 了 + 北京 去了北京	go+LE+north+capital have gone to Beijing	102/067/005/059/
不 + 去 + 北京 + 了 不去北京了	not going to Beijing anymore	007/102/005/059/067
天热了	sky + hot + LE the weather is getting hotter	128/103/067
她做妈妈了	she has become a mother	126/178/074/074/067
车来了	the bus is coming now	010/065/067
我天天吃了饭去学校	I + each day + after breakfast + go to school I go to school after breakfast every day	132/128/128/011/067/ 026/102/150/144
太多了	too much	127/023/067

Example Sentences

1/067	Chinese	我的医生不在这儿，他昨天去中国了。	
	English	My doctor is not here. He went to China yesterday.	
2/067	Chinese	我今天中午吃了中国饭，喝了中国茶。	
	English	Today at lunch, I had Chinese food and drank Chinese tea.	
3/067	Chinese	十二月了，天气冷了。	
	English	December has come. The weather is getting cold.	
4/067	Chinese	我天天都吃了午饭看书，看了书去商店工作。	
	English	Every day, I read after lunch. After I've finished reading, I go to work at in the shop.	
5/067	Chinese	电车来了，你们上车，我们明天见！	
	English	The tram is coming now, you should get on. See you tomorrow!	

冷 cold lěng 068 | L

Chinese	English	Character codes
冷 + 菜 冷菜	cold dishes	068/008
冷 + 天 冷天	chilly days	068/128
冷 + 水 冷水	cold water	068/120
冷气	cold air/air conditioning	068/098
很冷	very cold	043/068
人很冷	person with a frosty manner	104/043/068
冷了	getting colder	068/067
不冷不热	comfortable	007/068/007/103
饭菜冷了	the food is already cold	026/008/068/067

Example Sentences

1/068	Chinese	这些都是冷菜冷饭，我不想吃。
	English	All these dishes and foods are cold. I don't want to eat them.
2/068	Chinese	今天天气很不好，太冷了。
	English	The weather today is very bad — it's too cold!
3/068	Chinese	天气很好，不冷不热。
	English	The weather is really good, neither cold nor hot.
4/068	Chinese	这是冷菜，那是热菜，我们开吃好吗？
	English	These are cold dishes and those are hot. Shall we start eating?
5/068	Chinese	天气很热，我们没有冷气，很对不起！
	English	The weather is very hot, but we don't have air conditioning. I'm very sorry!

L | 069 里 in/inside/Chinese mile lǐ

Chinese	English	Character codes
里 + 面 里面	inside	069/081
三 + 里 三里	three Chinese miles	106/069
书 + 店 + 里 书店里	inside the bookshop	119/018/069
他的话里	from his words	125/015/046/069
在电话里	on the telephone	164/017/046/069
在电影里	in the film	164/017/156/069
那里	there	085/069
哪里	where	084/069
书里	in the book	119/069

Example Sentences

1/069	Chinese	谢医生在里面吗?
	English	Is Doctor Xie inside?
2/069	Chinese	小明在电话里说，他后天来我们家。
	English	Little Ming said by phone that he would come to our home the day after tomorrow.
3/069	Chinese	在这个电影里，有她的一个大学同学。
	English	In this film, there is one of her fellow university students.
4/069	Chinese	我前天在书店里买了一本很好的小说。
	English	The day before yesterday, I bought a very nice novel in this bookshop.
5/069	Chinese	书里面说，中国的东北很大。是吗?
	English	The book said China's Northeast is very large. Is that correct?

亮 shine/bright liàng 070 L

Chinese	English	Character codes
漂 + 亮 漂亮	clean+bright pretty	093/070
天 + 亮 + 了 天亮了	the sky became light	128/070/067
天 + 没 + 亮 天没亮	the sky is not yet light	128/078/070
亮亮的	glittering/sparkling	070/070/015
亮不亮?	bright or not	070/007/070

Example Sentences

1/070	Chinese	他们的学校很漂亮。	
	English	Their school is very beautiful.	
2/070	Chinese	这个院子很大，很漂亮。	
	English	This courtyard is very big and very beautiful.	
3/070	Chinese	天亮了，我们出去好不好？	
	English	It's light already. Shall we go out?	
4/070	Chinese	我有一个中国朋友，他天天都是天不亮起来读书。	
	English	I have a Chinese friend who gets up every day before sunrise to study.	
5/070	Chinese	这儿亮，那儿不亮，我们在这儿学习好不好？	
	English	Here it's bright, but there it isn't bright. Shall we move over here to study?	

L | 071 零 zero líng

Chinese	English	Character codes
二零零四 + 年 二零零四年	(the year) 2004	025/071/071/123/090
零 + 钱 零钱	small change	071/100
零 + 买 零买	buy a small quantity	071/075
零吃	snacks	071/011
零工	casual work	071/032
零点	at 12 am	071/016
零星	a bit of	071/148
零点一七	0.17	071/016/152/095

Example Sentences

1/071	Chinese	我儿子一岁零两个月。	
	English	My son is one year and two months old.	
2/071	Chinese	这是五十块，对不起，我没有零钱。	
	English	Sorry to give you 50 yuan. I don't have any small change.	
3/071	Chinese	我在一家饭馆做一点儿零工，钱很少。	
	English	I am doing part-time work at a restaurant. It pays very little.	
4/071	Chinese	小谢二零一八年六月去中国北京三个月。	
	English	Little Xie went to Beijing, China in June 2018 and stayed for three months.	
5/071	Chinese	我星期六在一家商店做三个小时的零工，星期天在一家中国饭馆做下午的零工。	
	English	On Saturdays, I do three hours of part-time work in a shop. On Sundays, I do an afternoon part-time job in a Chinese restaurant.	

Chinese	English	Character codes
六 + 年 六年	six years	072/090
一九六六 + 年 一九六六年	(the year) 1966	152/060/072/072/090
六 + 个 + 月 六个月	six months	072/031/162
六个星期	six weeks	072/031/148/096
六点	six o'clock	072/016
二十六分钟	26 minutes	025/114/072/028/169
一块六	one *yuan* sixty *fen*	152/064/072
六个小时	six hours	072/031/143/115
零点一六	0.16	071/016/152/072

Example Sentences

1/071	Chinese	今天是九月六号，我来这家商店工作六年了。	
	English	Today is the 6th of September, and I have been working in the shop for Six years.	
2/071	Chinese	我妈妈一九六六年生在北京。	
	English	My mum was born in Beijing in 1966.	
3/071	Chinese	今天的电影是六点的 *。	
	English	Today the film is at 6 pm.	
4/071	Chinese	我坐明天上午十点十六分的火车去北京。	
	English	I will take the 10:16 am train to Beijing tomorrow.	
5/071	Chinese	大苹果一块六一个，你买不买？	
	English	These large apples cost one *yuan* and sixty *fen* each. Do you want to buy them or not?	

M | 073 吗 grammatical code ma

Chinese	English	Character codes
你 + 喝 + 茶 + 吗 你喝茶吗？	Do you drink tea?	089/041/009/073
天 + 气 + 好 + 吗 天气好吗？	Is the weather good?	128/098/039/073
这 + 里 + 是 + 书 + 店 + 吗 这里是书店吗？	Is this a bookshop?	167/069/118/119/018/073
她是老师吗？	Is she a teacher?	126/118/066/113/073
你在饭馆儿里吗？	Are you in the restaurant?	089/164/026/ 035/024/069/073
有人吗？	Is anybody there?	158/104/073
是吗？	Really?	118/073

Example Sentences

1/073	Chinese	今天的天气很热，是吗？
	English	It's very hot today, isn't it?
2/073	Chinese	你是他们的老师吗？
	English	Are you their teacher?
3/073	Chinese	我们今天不出去，明天出去好吗？
	English	Today we didn't go out. How about going out tomorrow?
4/073	Chinese	明天你们家里有人吗？我上午十点去好吗？
	English	Will someone be at your home tomorrow? Would it be alright if I go to your home tomorrow morning at 10?
5/073	Chinese	这个中国饭馆很好吗？他们做的菜好吃吗？
	English	Is this Chinese restaurant good? Is the food they cook good?

Chinese	English	Character codes
妈 + 妈 妈妈	mum	074/074
我 + 妈妈 我妈妈	my mother	132/074/074
妈妈 + 做 + 的 + 饭 妈妈做的饭	the food my mum made	074/074/178/015/026
爸爸和妈妈	daddy and mummy	003/003/042/074/074
后妈	stepmother	044/074

Example Sentences

1/074	Chinese	我妈妈昨天来北京了。	
	English	My mum came to Beijing yesterday.	
2/074	Chinese	我朋友的妈妈是医生。	
	English	My friend's mum is a doctor.	
3/074	Chinese	妈妈想买的衣服不在这个商店，在那个商店。	
	English	The clothes my mum would like to buy are not from this shop but that one.	
4/074	Chinese	在我们大学，很多同学的爸爸妈妈都是中国人。	
	English	At our university, a lot of our fellow students' dads and mums are Chinese.	
5/074	Chinese	我是九月十六号那天出生的。妈妈、爸爸和姐姐三个人都来了，那天我很高兴。	
	English	The 16th of September is my birthday. My mum, dad and elder sister are all coming here, so I were very happy that day.	

M | 075 买 buy mǎi

Chinese	English	Character codes
买 + 什 + 么 买什么？	buy what	075/111/077
买 + 不 + 买 买不买？	buy or not	075/007/075
买 + 了 + 吗 买了吗？	already bought or not yet?	075/067/073
不买了	won't buy	007/075/067
我买了三本书。	I bought three books	132/075/067/106/006/119

Example Sentences

1/075	Chinese	我很喜欢买书。
	English	I really like to buy books.
2/075	Chinese	明天我买菜，你做饭怎么样?
	English	Tomorrow I will buy ingredients to make food and you can cook. What do you think?
3/075	Chinese	我买的衣服是这个商店的，很好看，不是吗?
	English	The clothes I bought from this shop are very pretty, aren't they?
4/075	Chinese	A：苹果零买是一块五一个，你买几个? B：我买三个。 A：三个是四块五。
	English	A. Each apple is 1.5 yuan. How many do you want to buy? B. I want to buy three. A. 4.5 yuan for three.
5/075	Chinese	对不起，这个桌子和那个椅子我不买了，我没有那么多钱。
	English	Sorry, I can't buy this table and that chair. I don't have that much money.

猫 cat māo **076** | **M**

Chinese	English	Character codes
小 + 猫 小猫	small cat	143/076
老 + 猫 老猫	old cat	066/076
漂 + 亮 + 的 + 猫 漂亮的猫	pretty cat	093/070/015/076
我买的猫	the cat I bought	132/075/015/076
谁的猫？	Whose cat?	110/015/076
看见了一个猫	have seen a cat	062/054/067/152/031/076

Example Sentences

1/076	Chinese	这小猫是你们家的吗？
	English	Does this kitten belong to your family?
2/076	Chinese	猫和狗不很友好。
	English	Cats and dogs are not good friends.
3/076	Chinese	椅子上的那个猫的名字叫"来来"。
	English	That cat sitting on the chair is called Lailai.
4/076	Chinese	你的猫什么时候睡觉？
	English	What time does your cat go to sleep?
5/076	Chinese	我妈妈太喜欢猫了，这些猫都是她的。
	English	My mum loves cats so much. All these cats belong to her.

M | 077 么 What suffix me

Chinese	English	Character codes
什 + 么 什么	what	111/077
怎 + 么 怎么	how/why/what	165/077
怎么 + 样 怎么样	how about	165/077/151
这么	so/such/in this way/like this	167/077
那么	so/such/like that/in that way	085/077
那么点儿	so little/so few	085/077/016/024

Example Sentences

1/077	Chinese	A：你说什么? B：我没有说什么。
	English	A: What did you say? B: I didn't say anything.
2/077	Chinese	一点了，你怎么不去吃午饭?
	English	It is 1 o'clock. Why aren't you going to have lunch?
3/077	Chinese	天气那么冷，我们不去看电影了，好不好?
	English	Since the weather is so cold, let's not go out to watch a film. Is that OK with you?
4/077	Chinese	谢医生怎么样? 他回医院了吗?
	English	How is Doctor Xie? Has he returned to the hospital?
5/077	Chinese	那么点儿钱，我们什么都不能买。
	English	We have so little money. We cannot buy anything.

没 not have / disappear méi 078 | M

Chinese	English	Character codes
没 + 有 没有	do not have	078/158
没 + 了 没（有）了	don't have anymore / disappeared	078/(158)/067
没 + 喝 没喝	didn't drink	078/041
没钱	do not have money/poor	078/100
没工作	don't have a job/unemployed	078/032/176
没在饭馆	isn't in the restaurant	078/164/026/035
没冷气	does not have air conditioning	078/068/098
没见朋友	didn't meet friends	078/054/092/157
没什么	it's nothing	078/111/077
没看见	didn't see	078/062/054
没关系	doesn't matter	078/034/138

Example Sentences

1/078	Chinese	我昨天没来，我能不能明天中午来？	
	English	I didn't come yesterday. Can I come at noon tomorrow?	
2/078	Chinese	雨这么大，我们不能没有雨衣。	
	English	The rain is so heavy. We cannot go out without a raincoat.	
3/078	Chinese	我们星期一的工作很多，你怎么没来？	
	English	We were very busy on Monday, why didn't you come?	
4/078	Chinese	A: 我们昨天没看电视，今天的天气怎么样？ B: 昨天电视上说，今天中午会下大雨。	
	English	A: We didn't watch television yesterday. What is the weather today? B: Yesterday on the television they said today we would have heavy rain at noon.	
5/078	Chinese	这家书店里没有汉语书，我们去那家看看他们那里有没有。	
	English	There are no Chinese books in this bookshop. Let's go to that one to see if they have any.	

M | 079 们 plural for mankind / pronouns and nouns men

Chinese	English	Character codes
我 + 们 我们	we/us	132/079
你 + 们 你们	you	089/079
他 + 们 他们	they/them	125/079
朋友们	friends	092/157/079
工人们	workers	032/104/079
老师们	teachers	066//113/079

Example Sentences

1/079	Chinese	我们都不是中国人，没有人会说汉语。	
	English	None of us are Chinese. None of us are able to speak Chinese.	
2/079	Chinese	朋友们都来了，我们现在开饭好吗？	
	English	Our friends have all arrived. Let's start serving the food, how about it?	
3/079	Chinese	大家都说好了，他们三个女同学住在上面，我们六个住在下面。	
	English	We have all agreed: those three female students will live upstairs and the six of us will live downstairs.	
4/079	Chinese	谢老师说："老师们，同学们，今天开学了，我很高兴！你们呢？"	
	English	Teacher Xie says, 'Teachers and students, today is the first day of the new term. I am very happy! How about you?'	
5/079	Chinese	工人们都来了，现在开工！	
	English	As all the workers are here, we should start work now!	

米 rice/metre mǐ **080** **M**

Chinese	English	Character codes
大 + 米 大米	rice	014/080
小 + 米 小米	millet	143/080
米 + 饭 米饭	cooked rice	080/026
做米饭	to cook rice	178/080/026
十米	ten metres	114/080

Example Sentences

1/080	Chinese	今天中午我来做菜，你做米饭怎么样？
	English	For lunch today, I will cook the dishes and you can cook the rice. What do you think?
2/080	Chinese	他很高，有一米九！
	English	He is quite tall, around one metre and ninety centimetres!
3/080	Chinese	明天我请同学们吃饭，我现在去买一些大米。
	English	I invited my fellow students to dinner tomorrow. Now I must go to buy some rice.
4/080	Chinese	他说他不喜欢天天吃面，他很想吃吃米饭。
	English	He says he doesn't want to eat noodles every day. He'd really like to eat some rice.
5/080	Chinese	我们去一家北京饭馆儿好吗？那儿有很好吃的北京菜，有米饭也有面。
	English	Shall we go to a Beijing-style restaurant? There, you will find some good Beijing food. There will be both rice and noodles.

M | 081 面 flour/noodle/face/side miàn

Chinese	English	Character codes
吃 + 面 吃面	eat noodles	011/081
面 + 点 面点	pastry	081/016
面 + 店 面店	noodle shop	081/018
面前	in front	081/099
里面	inside	069/081
面子	face/outer part	081/172

Example Sentences

1/081	Chinese	北京人大都很喜欢吃面。
	English	Most Beijing people love to eat noodles.
2/081	Chinese	这个饭馆儿是一个面店，没有米饭吃。
	English	This restaurant is a noodle shop. There is no rice to eat here.
3/081	Chinese	在爸爸妈妈面前他是一个好儿子，在学生面前他是一个好老师。他是一个很好很好的人！
	English	To his parents, he is a good son; to his students, he is a good teacher. He truly is a really good person!
4/081	Chinese	他在我前面，你在我后面，好不好？
	English	He is in front of me and you are behind me. Is that alright?
5/081	Chinese	中国人很爱面子，做什么都喜欢有面子。
	English	Chinese people are very concerned with saving face. Whatever they do, they want to save face.

Chinese	English	Character codes
名 + 字 名字	name	082/173
有 + 名 有名	famous	158/082
名 + 人 名人	celebrity	082/104
名店	famous shop	082/018
名气	fame	082/098
人名	person's name	104/082
书名	name of a book	119/052
店名	shop name	018/082

Example Sentences

1/082	Chinese	我的名字是谢国明。你叫什么名字?
	English	My name is Xie Guoming. What is your name?
2/082	Chinese	这家医院很有名气。
	English	This hospital is quite famous.
3/082	Chinese	我昨天买了一本做菜的书，书名是《北京菜》。
	English	Yesterday I bought a cookbook. It is named *Beijing Food*.
4/082	Chinese	我认识的一些有钱人，他们去名商店买衣服，去名饭馆吃饭，开名车，喜欢和名人做朋友，有名狗和名猫，他们喜欢什么都有名。
	English	I know some wealthy people who always go to famous shops to buy clothes, eat at famous restaurants, drive brand-name cars, enjoy being friends with celebrities and have pedigree dogs and cats. In other words, they like everything to be a brand.
5/082	Chinese	明天我们看的电影叫什么名字? 是不是那个叫《飞人》的电影?
	English	What is the name of the film we will watch tomorrow? Is it the one called *The Flying Person*?

M | 083 明 bright/sight/understand/tomorrow míng

Chinese	English	Character codes
明 + 天 明天	tomorrow	083/128
天 + 明 天明	daybreak	128/083
明 + 亮 明亮	bright	083/070
明明	obviously	083/083
明星	film star or celebrity	083/148
说明	explain	122/083
不明	not clear	007/083
明年	next year	083/090
明了（liǎo）	clear	083/067

Example Sentences

1/083	Chinese	明天谁来我们家？
	English	Who will come to our home tomorrow?
2/083	Chinese	他是有名的电影明星。
	English	He is a famous film star.
3/083	Chinese	我喜欢这家商店，里面很明亮，很漂亮。
	English	I like this shop because it is bright and pretty inside.
4/083	Chinese	我的朋友们都很爱学习，他们天天都在天明的时候学汉语。
	English	All my friends love learning and they study Chinese at daybreak each day.
5/083	Chinese	你明明看见了，怎么说没看见？
	English	You clearly did see it. Why did you say that you didn't see it?

Chinese	English	Character codes
哪 + 里 哪里	where	084/069
哪 + 儿 哪儿	where	084/024
哪 + 面 哪面	which side	084/081
哪年	which year	084/090
哪个星期	which week	084/031/150/096
哪里人	person from which place	084/069/104
哪儿都去	go all places	084/024/020/102
那儿是哪儿？	where is there	085/024/118/084/024

Example Sentences

1/084	Chinese	我们叫的出租车在哪里？
	English	Where is the taxi we booked?
2/084	Chinese	你哪年哪月去北京？
	English	Which year and month do you go to Beijing?
3/084	Chinese	A：你说是那儿，那儿是哪儿？ B：我说的"那儿"是商店前面的中学。
	English	A: You said 'there' but where do you mean? B: When I said 'there', I meant the middle school located in front of the shop.
4/084	Chinese	我不买他的苹果，他生气了，说："哪儿的苹果都没有我这儿的好！"
	English	After I did not buy his apples, he got angry and said, 'Nowhere else will you find apples as good as mine!'
5/084	Chinese	我听说，你今年九月不能上这个大学了，是吗？你去哪个大学？
	English	I have heard that you cannot go to this university in September this year. Is it true? Which university will you go to?

N | 085 那 that nà; nèi

Chinese	English	Character codes
那 + 里 那里	there; over there; that place	085/069
那 + 儿 那儿	there; over there; that place	085/024
那 + 面 那面	that side	085/081
那么	such; so; then; anyway	085/077
那么热	so hot	085/077/103
那么一点儿	so little	085/077/152/016/024
那时	at that time/moment	085/115
那是什么？	What is that?	085/118/111/077
那个人是谁？	Who is that man?	085/031/104/118/110
那怎么样？	So what?	085/165/077/151
那天	that day	085/128
那个星期	that week	085/031/148/096
那年	that year	085/090

Example Sentences

1/085	Chinese	那里的人都是北京来的。	
	English	All the people over there are from Beijing.	
2/085	Chinese	谢医生来北京的那个星期，我不在北京。	
	English	The week Doctor Xie comes to Beijing, I won't be in Beijing.	
3/085	Chinese	他们都说那里好，是吗？怎么好？	
	English	All of them say that place is good, is it? How good is it?	
4/085	Chinese	我认识小明的那天是上个星期六，在中国饭馆。	
	English	The day I met Little Ming was last Saturday at a Chinese restaurant.	
5/085	Chinese	我是三十年前去北京的，那时北京不那么热。	
	English	I went to Beijing 30 years ago. At that time, the weather was not so hot.	

Chinese	English	Character codes
大 + 脑 大脑	brain	014/086
小 + 脑 小脑	cerebellum	143/086
脑 + 子 脑子	brain	086/172
没脑子	brainless, foolish, stupid, muddled	078/086/172
电脑	computer	017/086
做电脑的	the computer maker	178/017/086/015
开电脑	switch on computer	061/017/086
上电脑	use a computer	108/017/086
做电脑的工作	computer professionals	017/086/015/032/176

Example Sentences

1/086	Chinese	我不想买这个电脑，太老了。	
	English	I don't want to buy this computer. The model is too old.	
2/086	Chinese	对不起，我脑子不好，不认识这个汉字了。	
	English	I am sorry. I have a poor memory, so I cannot recognise this Chinese character now.	
3/086	Chinese	小明的爸爸开了一个电脑店，我们去看看好吗？	
	English	Little Ming's father opened a computer shop. Shall we go and have a look around it?	
4/086	Chinese	看，你的书在你的桌子上，没脑子！	
	English	Look! Your book is on your table. You have such a poor memory!	
5/086	Chinese	开开你的电脑好吗？我想上去看看有没有我想买的书。	
	English	Could you switch on your computer? I'd like to use it to find the book I want to buy.	

N | 087 呢 grammatical code / question code ne

Chinese	English	Character codes
我认识他，你呢？	I know him. Do you?	132/105/116/125, 089/087
他没有钱，你呢？	He doesn't have money. Do you?	125/078/158/100, 089/087
今天不买，明天呢？	Today I will not buy it. Maybe tomorrow?	058/128/007/075, 083/128/087
我是北京人，他们呢？	I am a Beijinger. Are they?	132/118/005/059/104, 125/079/087
我看，你呢？	I will watch (it). Will you?	132/062, 089/087
现在我们吃午饭，午饭后呢？	Now we will eat lunch. How about after lunch?	141/164/132/079/011/134/026, 134/026/044/087

Example Sentences

1/087	Chinese	我们今天是朋友，明天呢？
	English	We are friends today. How about tomorrow?
2/087	Chinese	你爸爸是西北人，你妈妈呢？
	English	Your father comes from the Northwest. How about your mother?
3/087	Chinese	我睡觉了，你呢？
	English	I will go to bed soon. What about you?
4/087	Chinese	这个书店没有你想买的书，那个书店呢？
	English	This bookshop does not have the book you want. How about that (other) bookshop?
5/087	Chinese	你的东西椅子上没有，桌子上呢？
	English	Your things are not on the chair. Are they on the table?

能 ability / capability / energy néng 088 | N

Chinese	English	Character codes
很 + 能 很能	very capable	043/088
不 + 很能 不很能	not very capable	007/043/088
能 + 不 + 能 能不能？	can or cannot?	088/007/088
能吃	able to eat	088/011
能说	able to say	088/122
能写	able to write	088/146
想能	hope to be able to	142/088
能人	capable person	088/104
电能	electric power	017/088

Example Sentences

1/088	Chinese	你明天能来吗？
	English	Can you come tomorrow?
2/088	Chinese	我姐姐很能做中国菜！
	English	My elder sister is very good at cooking Chinese food.
3/088	Chinese	你今年十六岁，不能上大学。
	English	You are 16 years old this year, so you cannot start university.
4/088	Chinese	我们能不能不坐火车去东北，我们开车去好不好？
	English	Can we not go by train to the Northeast and drive instead?
5/088	Chinese	我昨天认识的那个能说汉语的人，你认识吗？
	English	That person I got to know yesterday is able to speak Chinese. Do you know him?

N | 089 你 you nǐ

Chinese	English	Character codes
你 + 的 你的	your/yours	089/015
你 + 们 你们	you	089/079
你们 + 的 你们的	your/yours	089/079/015
坐你们的车	ride in your car	177/089/079/015/010
你我是好朋友	You and I are good friends.	089/132/118/039/092/157

Example Sentences

1/089	Chinese	你的朋友能说汉语吗？
	English	Can your friend speak Chinese?
2/089	Chinese	我坐你们的车去看电影好吗?
	English	Can I ride in your car to go see the film?
3/089	Chinese	你我是十年的好朋友了。
	English	You and I have been good friends for ten years.
4/089	Chinese	你的苹果十五块钱三个？我没有那么多钱，我不买了。
	English	Your apples are 15 *yuan* for three? I don't have that much money, so I won't buy them.
5/089	Chinese	你看我，我看你，我们四个人谁都没有钱。
	English	You're looking at me, and I'm looking at you. Of the four of us, none have any money.

Chinese	English	Character codes
二零零四 + 年 二零零四 年	(the year) 2004	025/071/071/123/090
年 + 年 年年	each year	090/090
年 + 饭 年饭	New Year's dinner	090/026
好年	a good year	039/090
少 * 年	early youth	109/090
年前	by the end of this year	090/099
前年	the year before last year	099/090
年后	at the beginning of next year	090/044
后年	the year after next	044/090
大后年	three years from now	014/ 044/090
明年	next year	083/090

注释 Note

* 少 shǎo=young

Example Sentences

1/090	Chinese	今年是 2019 年。	
	English	This year it's 2019.	
2/090	Chinese	米医生年年都来北京医院工作三个月。	
	English	Every year Doctor Mi comes to Beijing Hospital to work for three months.	
3/090	Chinese	老谢说，他明年不开出租车了，他想开一个中国饭馆。	
	English	Old Xie says he won't drive a taxi anymore next year. He wants to open a Chinese restaurant.	
4/090	Chinese	我今年三月来北京，明年四月回东北，在北京住一年。	
	English	In March this year I will go to Beijing, and I will return to the Northeast next year in April. So I will live in Beijing for one year.	
5/090	Chinese	我妈妈说，她三年没去北京了，她很想北京。	
	English	My mother says she has not been to Beijing for three years and she really misses it.	

N | 091 女 female/woman nǚ

Chinese	English	Character codes
女 + 人 女人	women	091/104
女 + 朋友 女朋友	female + friend girlfriend	091/092/157
女 + 工 女工	woman worker	091/032
女子	woman	091/172
女星	female star	091/148
女生	female student	091/112
女儿	daughter	091/024
儿女	children (to the parents)	024/091
女气	woman + air effeminate	091/098

Example Sentences

1/091	Chinese	这些人都是女工。	
	English	These people are all female workers.	
2/091	Chinese	我们学校的女生很多。	
	English	There are many female students in our school.	
3/091	Chinese	昨天他妈妈生了一个女儿。	
	English	Yesterday his mum gave birth to a daughter.	
4/091	Chinese	我女朋友说，她昨天在电影院看的电影很好。	
	English	My girlfriend said that the movie she watched at the cinema yesterday was very good.	
5/091	Chinese	现在我们大学的一个女生是电影明星。	
	English	One of the female students from our university is now a film star.	

朋 gang up/friend/pal péng 092 | P

Chinese	English	Character codes
朋 + 友 朋友	buddy+friendly friend	092/157
好 + 朋友 好朋友	good friend	039/092/157
女 + 朋友 女朋友	girlfriend	091/092/157
小朋友	kids	143/092/157
老朋友	old/good friend	066/092/157
是朋友	to be a friend	118/092/157
医院的朋友	the friend who works at a hospital	154/161/015/092/157
我认识的朋友	the friend I recognise	132/105/116/015/092/157
电脑上的朋友	net friend	017/086/108/015/092/157

Example Sentences

1/092	Chinese	小明的女朋友是北京人。
	English	Little Ming's girlfriend is a Beijinger.
2/092	Chinese	大谢今天很漂亮，听说是去见女朋友。
	English	Big Xie looks very handsome today. I heard he was going to see his girlfriend.
3/092	Chinese	我今天中午在一家北京的饭馆儿请我东北来的朋友吃饭。
	English	Today at noon I will invite my friends who have travelled from the Northeast to dine at a Beijing restaurant.
4/092	Chinese	我昨天认识了一个在北京的医院工作的朋友。
	English	Yesterday I got to know a friend who works at a hospital in Beijing.
5/092	Chinese	我爸爸妈妈都很不喜欢我在电脑上认识的朋友。
	English	My father and mother don't like the friends I met online.

P | 093 漂 floating piāo; beautiful piào

Chinese	English	Character codes
漂 + 亮 漂亮	clean + bright pretty	093/070
漂 + 漂 + 亮 + 亮 漂漂亮亮	nice-looking	093/093/070/070
漂亮 + 话 漂亮话	fine words	093/070/046
漂（piāo）在水上	float on water	093/164/120/108

Example Sentences

1/093	Chinese	这个椅子很漂亮。
	English	This chair is quite pretty.
2/093	Chinese	你的家漂漂亮亮的，很好。
	English	Your home is nice-looking. It's really nice!
3/093	Chinese	我不喜欢爱说漂亮话的人。
	English	I don't like people who are sweet talkers.
4/093	Chinese	这个东西在水上漂来漂去好儿天了。
	English	This object has been floating in the water for many days.
5/093	Chinese	你认识我们汉语老师的那个很漂亮的女朋友吗?
	English	Do you know that pretty woman who is our Chinese teacher's girlfriend?

苹 apple píng 094 | P

Chinese	English	Character codes
苹 + 果 苹果	apple	094/037
好 + 苹果 好苹果	good apples	039/094/037
苹果 + 好 + 吃 苹果好吃	the apples are delicious	094/037/039/011
好吃的苹果	the delicious apples	039/011/015/094/037
中国的苹果	the apples from China	168/036/015/094/037
上午吃的苹果	the apples for eating in the morning	108/134/011/015/094/037
一些苹果	some apples	152/145/094/037
不大不小的苹果	the medium-sized apples	007/014/007/143/015/094/037
水果店的苹果	the apples in the fruit shop	120/037/018/ 015/094/037

Example Sentences

1/094	Chinese	我前天买的苹果很好吃。	
	English	The apples I bought the day before yesterday were delicious.	
2/094	Chinese	这几个苹果多少钱?	
	English	How much do these few apples cost?	
3/094	Chinese	我们明天去谢老师的家，我们买一些苹果好吗?	
	English	As we will go to Teacher Xie's home tomorrow, should we buy some apples?	
4/094	Chinese	那个水果店里的水果很多，我们是十个人，买十个苹果吃，一个人一个好不好?	
	English	There is a lot of fruit in that fruit shop. We are ten people and we'll buy ten apples to eat so that each person will get one. Is that alright?	
5/094	Chinese	大家都说中国的苹果很好吃，我中午吃了一个，是很好吃，我明天想再买一些。	
	English	Everyone says apples from China are delicious. I ate one at noon and it was tasty, so I would like to buy some more tomorrow.	

Q 095 七 seven qī

Chinese	English	Character codes
七 + 块 + 钱 七块钱	seven + MW+ money seven *kuai*	095/064/100/
七 + 天 七天	seven days	095/128
七 + 月 + 十七 + 号 七月十七号	July 17	095/162/114/095/040
七点	seven o'clock	095/016
七个水果	seven fruits	095/031/120/037
七杯茶	seven cups of tea	095/004/009
七个老师	seven teachers	095/031/066/113
火车上午七点零七开。	The train's departure time is 7:07 a.m.	050/010/108/134/095/ 016/071/095/061

Example Sentences

1/095	Chinese	谢老师上午七点来。	
	English	Teacher Xie will arrive at 7 a.m.	
2/095	Chinese	今天来开会的人很多，有七八十个人。	
	English	Today there are a lot of people coming to the meeting, about 70 or 80 people.	
3/095	Chinese	我们看明天早晨七点的电视，好吗？	
	English	Shall we watch the television program at 7 a.m. tomorrow?	
4/095	Chinese	车七点来，现在五点，我们看看电视好吗？	
	English	The bus arrives at 7 o'clock. It's 5 o'clock now. Shall we watch television?	
5/095	Chinese	这个桌子七十五块，椅子十七块，我们有钱买吗？	
	English	This table costs 75 *yuan*. The chair is 17 *yuan*. Do we have enough money to purchase them?	

期 a period of time / phase qī 096 | Q

Chinese	English	Character codes
星 + 期 星期	star + period week	148/096
学 + 期 学期	study + period school term	150/096
时 + 期 时期	period of time	115/096
工期	time limit for a project	032/096

Example Sentences

1/096	Chinese	这个学期我们有很多学生。	
	English	We have a lot of students this term.	
2/096	Chinese	同学们七月七号星期三去西北。	
	English	Students will go to the Northwest on wednesday the 7th of July.	
3/096	Chinese	汉语我们学习了三个学期了。	
	English	We have already studied Chinese for three terms.	
4/096	Chinese	谢小姐，今天是星期四，不是星期五。我们一会儿坐出租车去北京饭店，你去不去？	
	English	Miss Xie, today is Thursday, not Friday. We will take a taxi to Beijing Hotel shortly. Are you coming with us?	
5/096	Chinese	有些人这个学期不来了，明年再来。	
	English	Some people won't come this term. They will be back next year.	

Q 097 起 rise/begin qǐ

Chinese	English	Character codes
对 + 不 + 起 对不起	face to + not + up sorry	022/007/097
买 + 不 + 起 买不起	cannot afford to buy	075/007/097
看 + 不 + 起 看不起	look +not + up/worth despise	062/007/097
起来	rise + up get up; stand up	097/065
坐起来	sit+ rise + up sit up	177/097/065
想起来	think + rise + up recall; think of	142/097/065
读起来	read + rise + up begin to read	021/097/065
看起来	look + rise + up seem to; look like	062/097/065
听起来	listen + rise + up sound like	129/097/065
一起	together	152/097
在一起	stay together	164/152/097
一起去	go together	152/097/102

Example Sentences

1/097	Chinese	对不起，我不和你一起去了。	
	English	I'm sorry, but I cannot go with you.	
2/097	Chinese	这么好的衣服，我买不起。	
	English	This dress is too good, I cannot afford it.	
3/097	Chinese	他看起来不太高兴。	
	English	He looks unhappy.	
4/097	Chinese	看起来，这本书很好。	
	English	This book seems very good.	
5/097	Chinese	A: 你想起来了吗？他叫什么名字？ B: 我想起来了，他叫米大明。	
	English	A: Do you remember what his name is? B: Yes, I remember now. His name is Mi Daming.	

Chinese	English	Character codes
客 + 气 客气	customer+air polite/courteous	063/098
不 + 客 + 气 不客气	no+customer+air you're welcome	007/063/098
天 + 气 天气	sky+air weather	128/098
好天气	good+sky+air good weather	039/128/098
生气	grow+air get angry	112/098
语气	language +air tone	160/098
小气	small+air stingy	143/098
大气	big+air generous	014/098
和气	harmony + air gentle/nice	042/098

Example Sentences

1/098	Chinese	A：谢谢你。 B：不客气!
	English	A: Thank you. B: You're welcome!
2/098	Chinese	今天天气很好。
	English	The weather is good today.
3/098	Chinese	他是个小气的人。
	English	He is a very stingy person.
4/098	Chinese	我们的汉语老师很和气。
	English	Our Chinese teacher is very nice.
5/098	Chinese	小明不好好学习，他妈妈很生气。
	English	Little Ming does not study hard enough, so his mum gets angry.

Q | 099 前 front/before/last qián

Chinese	English	Character codes
前 + 天 前天	before +day the day before yesterday	099/128
前 + 天 + 上 + 午 前天上午	before +day+up + the middle of the day morning of the day before yesterday	099/128/108/134
前 + 年 前年	before +year the year before last	099/090
前面	front+side in front of	099/081
桌子前面	desk+ suffix+front+side in front of the table	171/172/099/081
学校前面	in front of the school	150/144/099/081
面前	face +front before; facing; in front of	081/099

Example Sentences

1/099	Chinese	我是前年来的中国。	
	English	I came to China the year before last.	
2/099	Chinese	商店在学校的前面。	
	English	The shop is in front of the school.	
3/099	Chinese	老师站在桌子前面。	
	English	The teacher is standing in front of the table.	
4/099	Chinese	学校的前面有一个车站。	
	English	There is a bus stop in front of the school.	
5/099	Chinese	我前天上午去商店买了一点儿水果。	
	English	The day before yesterday in the morning, I went to the store and bought some fruit.	

钱 money qián 100 | Q

Chinese	English	Character codes
有 + 钱 有钱	have+money have money	158/100
有 + 钱 + 人 有钱人	have+money+people the rich	158/100/104
没 + 有 + 钱 没有钱	no+have +money have no money	078/158/100
多少钱	much+less +money how much	023/109/100
三块钱	three+measure word for piece + money three *yuan*	106/064/100
工钱	work+money wage	032/100

Example Sentences

1/100	Chinese	他爸爸是一个名医，人家都说，他会很有钱。
	English	His father is a famous doctor and everyone says that he will be very rich.
2/100	Chinese	A: 这本书多少钱？ B: 十五块钱。
	English	A: How much is this book? B: Fifteen *yuan*.
3/100	Chinese	这衣服我是八十块钱买的。
	English	I bought this dress for eighty *yuan*.
4/100	Chinese	我昨天在火车站认识的那个人不是一个有钱人，他说他现在没有工作了。
	English	The man I met at the train station is not a rich man. He said he lost his job.
5/100	Chinese	今天是三十一号，我们现在没有钱买电视机。
	English	Today is the 31st of the month, and we currently don't have enough money to buy a television.

Q 101 请 please/invite qǐng

Chinese	English	Character codes
请 + 客 请客	invite + guest treat	101/063
请 + 你 + 吃 + 饭 请你吃饭	invite + you + eat + food invite you to dinner	101/089/011/026
请 + 吃 请吃	invite + eat eat please	101/011
请喝	invite + drink drink please	101/041
请喝茶	invite + drink + tea drink some tea please	101/041/009
请看	invite + look please take a look	101/062
请坐	invite + sit sit down please	101/177
回请	return + invite give a return banquet	048/101

Example Sentences

1/101	Chinese	请看这里。	
	English	Please look here.	
2/101	Chinese	请打开书。	
	English	Please open your book.	
3/101	Chinese	请关上电视。	
	English	Please turn off the TV.	
4/101	Chinese	请吃一点儿水果。	
	English	Please eat some fruit.	
5/101	Chinese	今天他的大学同学来，不是我的，下午是他请客。	
	English	This afternoon he will pay the bill because the visiting friends are his university friends, not mine.	

去 leave/go qù **102** Q

Chinese	English	Character codes
回 + 去 回去	back + go go back	048/102
出 + 去 出去	out + go go out	012/102
去 + 北 + 京 去北京	go + north + capital go to Beijing	102/005/059
去商店	go + trade + shop go to a store	102/107/018
去学校	go + study + school go to school	102/150/144
去医院	go + medicine + yard go to hospital	102/154/161
去工作	go + job + work go to work	102/032/176
去学习	go + study + practice go to learn	102/150/136
去吃饭	go + eat + food go to have a meal	102/011/026
去做饭	go + do + food go to cook	102/178/026
去看电影	go + see + electricity + film go to see a movie	102/062/017/156

Example Sentences

1/102	Chinese	我上个月去北京了。
	English	I went to Beijing last month.
2/102	Chinese	你不能出去。
	English	You can't go out.
3/102	Chinese	我下午去商店买东西。
	English	I will go shopping this afternoon.
4/102	Chinese	我明天回去工作。
	English	I'll go back to work tomorrow.
5/102	Chinese	我们昨天下午去看电影了。
	English	We went to see a movie yesterday afternoon.

R | 103 热 hot heat rè

Chinese	English	Character codes
热 + 爱 热爱	hot + love love ardently	103/001
热 + 爱 + 学 + 习 热爱学习	hot + love + study + practice love to learn	103/001/150/136
热 + 狗 热狗	hot + dog hot dog	103/033
热水	hot + water hot water	103/120
热饭	warm food	103/026
热热菜	reheat the dishes	103/103/008
很热	very hot	043/103

Example Sentences

1/103	Chinese	北京今天很热。	
	English	Beijing is very hot today.	
2/103	Chinese	中国人喜欢喝热开水。	
	English	Chinese people like to drink hot water.	
3/103	Chinese	我不喜欢吃热狗。	
	English	I don't like hot dogs.	
4/103	Chinese	我朋友很热爱学习。	
	English	My friend really loves to learn.	
5/103	Chinese	今天天气很热，你呢，你热不热?	
	English	Today the weather was very hot. What about you? Do you feel hot or not?	

Chinese	English	Character codes
打 + 人 打人	hit + person hit somebody	013/104
大 + 人 大人	big + people adult	014/104
工 + 人 工人	work + people worker	032/104
家人	family + people family member	053/104
人家	people + family other people	104/053
老人	old + people old people	066/104
女人	female + people woman	091/104
商人	business + people business people	107/104
中国人	Chinese people	168/036/104

Example Sentences

1/104	Chinese	我的汉语老师是中国人。
	English	My Chinese teacher is Chinese.
2/104	Chinese	不是商人都很喜欢钱。
	English	It is not true that all businessmen love money.
3/104	Chinese	我爸爸妈妈都是工人。
	English	My parents are both workers.
4/104	Chinese	我很爱我的家人。
	English	I love my family.
5/104	Chinese	昨天下午买椅子的那个人是我妈妈的医生。
	English	The person that bought the chairs yesterday afternoon is my mum's doctor.

R | 105 认 recognise/make out rèn

Chinese	English	Character codes
认 + 识 认识	know + recognise know	105/116
认 + 出 + 来 认出来	know + out + come recognise	105/012/065
认 + 不 + 出 + 来 认不出来	know + no + out + come can't recognise	105/007/012/065
认字	recognise + characters literacy	105/173
认生	recognise + new face be shy with strangers	105/112

Example Sentences

1/105	Chinese	很高兴认识你。
	English	Nice to meet you.
2/105	Chinese	我不认识高小姐。
	English	I don't know Miss Gao.
3/105	Chinese	我认识他三年了。
	English	I've known him for three years.
4/105	Chinese	我和大钱是在中国认识的。
	English	Big Qian and I met in China.
5/105	Chinese	我认识很多在饭馆工作的中国人。
	English	I know a lot of Chinese people who work in restaurants.

Chinese	English	Character codes
三 + 天 三天	three + day three days	106/128
三 + 点 三点	three + o'clock three o'clock	106/016
三 + 分 三分	three + minute three minutes	106/028
三年	three + year three years	106/090
三个人	three + measure word + people three people	106/031/104
三个月	three + measure word+month three months	106/031/162
三个苹果	three + measure word + apple + fruit three apples	106/031/094/037

Example Sentences

1/106	Chinese	现在三点三十分。
	English	The time now is thirty minutes past three.
2/106	Chinese	桌子上有三个苹果。
	English	There are three apples on the table.
3/106	Chinese	我女儿今年三岁。
	English	My daughter is three years old.
4/106	Chinese	我来中国三个月了。
	English	I've been in China for three months.
5/106	Chinese	我三月三号坐飞机去北京。
	English	I'm flying to Beijing on the 3rd of March.

S | 107 商 trade/discuss shāng

Chinese	English	Character codes
商 + 店 商店	trade + shop store	107/018
电 + 商 电商	electricity + trade e-commerce	017/107
商 + 人 商人	business + people businessman	107/104
商人气	businessman + air businessman airs	107/104/098
衣服商	clothier	153/029/107
商机	business+chance business opportunity	107/051

Example Sentences

1/107	Chinese	我爸爸是个商人。
	English	My father is a businessman.
2/107	Chinese	医院的前面是一家商店。
	English	In front of the hospital is a shop.
3/107	Chinese	我妈妈在商店工作。
	English	My mother works in a shop.
4/107	Chinese	我想去商店买点儿东西。
	English	I want to go to a store to buy something.
5/107	Chinese	这家商店开到下午四点。
	English	This shop closes at 4 o'clock in the afternoon.

上 up/above shàng **108** | S

Chinese	English	Character codes
上 + 面 上面	above + side above; on top of	108/081
桌 + 子 + 上 + 面 桌子上面	table + suffix + above + side on the table	171/172/108/081
上 + 午 上午	above + noon morning	108/134
关上	shut + up shut up; turn off	034/108
天上	sky + up in the sky	128/108
上学	above + learn go to school	108/150
上飞机	up + fly + machine boarding	108/027/051
上个月	up + measure word + month last month	108/031/162

Example Sentences

1/108	Chinese	小猫在椅子上面睡觉。
	English	The little cat is sleeping on the chair.
2/108	Chinese	大家关上电视去睡觉。
	English	Everyone, turn off the TV and go to sleep now.
3/108	Chinese	天上有很多在上飞机在飞。
	English	There are many planes flying in the sky.
4/108	Chinese	今天下雨，我不去上学了。
	English	It's raining today, so I'm not going to school.
5/108	Chinese	我要上飞机了，我在飞机上是不能打电话的。
	English	I need to board the plane now. While I am on the plane, I will not be able to use the mobile phone.

S | 109 少 few / little / lack shǎo; young shào

Chinese	English	Character codes
多 + 少 多少	much + less how many	023/109
多 + 少 + 钱 多少钱	much + less + money how much	023/109/100
少 + 吃 + 一 + 点 + 儿 少吃一点儿	less + eat + one + point +word suffix do not eat too much	109/011/152/016/024
少买一点儿	less + buy + one + point +word suffix do not buy too much	109/075/152/016/024
买少了	buy + less +grammatical code not buy enough	075/109/067

Example Sentences

1/109	Chinese	这些水果多少钱？	
	English	How much do these fruits cost?	
2/109	Chinese	一年有多少天？	
	English	How many days are there in a year?	
3/109	Chinese	这些苹果一起有多少个？	
	English	How many apples are there altogether?	
4/109	Chinese	少看一点儿电视好吗？	
	English	Can we watch a little less television?	
5/109	Chinese	我水果买少了，星期一和星期二没有的吃了。	
	English	I didn't buy enough fruit, so on Monday and Tuesday we will have nothing to eat.	

Chinese	English	Character codes
谁 + 的 谁的	who + of whose	110/015
谁 + 去 谁去	who + go who is going	110/102
是 + 谁 是谁	is + whom who is	118/110
不是谁	not is who no one	007/118/110
都是谁	all + are + who who are they	020/118/110
谁都是	who + all + is everyone is	110/020/118

Example Sentences

1/110	Chinese	这本书是谁的?
	English	Whose book is this?
2/110	Chinese	你明天和谁去看电影?
	English	Who will you go to the movies with tomorrow?
3/110	Chinese	你是谁? 我不认识你。
	English	Who are you? I don't know you.
4/110	Chinese	谁喜欢吃我今天买的东北苹果?
	English	Who likes to eat the apples from the Northeast that I bought today?
5/110	Chinese	谁先来谁先吃。
	English	First come, first served.

S | 111　什 prefix for what shén

Chinese	English	Character codes
什 + 么 什么	prefix for what + suffix to what what	111/077
什 + 么 + 时 + 候 什么时候	prefix to what + suffix to what +time+wait when	111/077/115/045

Example Sentences

1/111	Chinese	你叫什么名字？	
	English	What is your name?	
2/111	Chinese	你喜欢吃什么水果？	
	English	What kind of fruit do you like?	
3/111	Chinese	你在做什么呢？	
	English	What are you doing?	
4/111	Chinese	现在下雨了，你什么时候回家？	
	English	It is raining now, so what time will you go home?	
5/111	Chinese	你说昨天你看见了很多东西，你都看见了什么？	
	English	You said that you saw many things yesterday. What did you see?	

Chinese	English	Character codes
生 + 气 生气	generate + anger get angry	112/098
学 + 生 学生	learn + man student	150/112
师 + 生 师生	teacher + student teacher and student	113/112
生了儿子	give birth to a son	112/067/024/172
一生	one + life all one's life	152/112
生前	life + before before death	112/099

Example Sentences

1/112	Chinese	你是学生吗？	
	English	Are you a student?	
2/112	Chinese	学校里有多少个学生？	
	English	How many students are there in the school?	
3/112	Chinese	老师很生气。	
	English	The teacher is very angry.	
4/112	Chinese	我们师生关系很好。	
	English	We have good teacher-student relationship.	
5/112	Chinese	他爸爸生前是一个大医院的医生，去年人不在了。	
	English	His father was a doctor at a large hospital, but he died last year.	

S | 113 师 teacher／master shī

Chinese	English	Character codes
老 + 师 老师	senior + teacher teacher	066/113
我 + 的 + 老 + 师 我的老师	I+grammatical code + senior + teacher my teacher	132/015/066/113
医 + 师 医师	medicine+ teacher doctor	154/113
汉语老师	Chinese language + teacher Chinese teacher	038/160/066/113
大师	big+master great master	014/113

Example Sentences

1/113	Chinese	这是我的汉语老师。
	English	This is my Chinese teacher.
2/113	Chinese	我朋友的妈妈是中学老师。
	English	My friend's mother is a middle school teacher.
3/113	Chinese	老师叫我坐下。
	English	The teacher told me to sit down.
4/113	Chinese	老师的衣服很漂亮。
	English	The teacher's clothes are beautiful.
5/113	Chinese	老师今天看起来很高兴。
	English	The teacher looked very happy today.

Chinese	English	Character codes
十 + 二 十二	ten + two twelve	114/025
二 + 十 二十	two + ten twenty	025/114
十 + 天 十天	ten + day ten days	114/128
十点	ten + o'clock ten o'clock	114/016
十分	ten + minute ten minutes	114/028
十分钟	ten + minute + clock ten minutes	114/028/169
十年	ten + year ten years	114/090
十个人	ten + measure word + people ten people	114/031/104
十个月	ten + measure word + month ten months	114/031/162
十本书	ten + measure word + book ten books	114/006/119

Example Sentences

1/114	Chinese	我明天上午十点去医院。
	English	I'll go to the hospital at ten o'clock tomorrow morning.
2/114	Chinese	我昨天买了十个苹果。
	English	I bought ten apples yesterday.
3/114	Chinese	这个杯子十块钱。
	English	This cup costs ten *yuan*.
4/114	Chinese	我上个月看了十本书。
	English	I read ten books last month.
5/114	Chinese	今年是 2019 年，我妈妈今年六十岁了。
	English	It was 2019, and my mother was sixty years old.

S | 115　时　time / chance　shí

Chinese	English	Character codes
小 + 时 小时	small + time hour	143/115
时 + 候 时候	time + wait when	115/045
小 + 时 + 候 小时候	small+time+wait when one was a child	143/115/045
什么时候	when	111/077/115/045

Example Sentences

1/115	Chinese	我朋友小时候很漂亮。
	English	My friend was very pretty when she was a child.
2/115	Chinese	你什么时候去吃饭？
	English	When will you go out to eat?
3/115	Chinese	你明天什么时候在家？
	English	What time will you be home tomorrow?
4/115	Chinese	吃饭的时候不能说话。
	English	Don't talk while eating.
5/115	Chinese	我们回来的时候四点了。
	English	It was four o'clock when we came back.

Chinese	English	Character codes
认 + 识 认识	know +recognise know	105/116
识 + 字 识字	recognise+character literacy	116/173
见 + 识 见识	know +recognise knowledge	054/116
有见识	have+ knowledge very knowledgeable	158/054/116
识字本	character book	116/173/006

Example Sentences

1/116	Chinese	他不识字。	
	English	He can't read.	
2/116	Chinese	你是什么时候识字的？	
	English	When could you read?	
3/116	Chinese	他能认识很多汉字。	
	English	He can recognise many Chinese characters.	
4/116	Chinese	我和大谢是在中国认识的。	
	English	Big Xie and I met in China.	
5/116	Chinese	我认识一些在火车站工作的中国人。	
	English	I know some Chinese people who work in the train station.	

S | 117 视 vision / look / see shì

Chinese	English	Character codes
电 + 视 电视	electricity +vision television (TV)	017/117
电视 + 商 + 店 电视商店	TV shop	017/117/107/018
看电视	watch TV	062/017/117
打开电视	turn on the TV	013/061/017/117
关上电视	turn off the TV	034/108/017/117

Example Sentences

1/117	Chinese	妈妈喜欢下午看电视。
	English	My mother likes to watch TV in the afternoon.
2/117	Chinese	电视在桌子上。
	English	The TV is on the table.
3/117	Chinese	我看了四十分钟电视。
	English	I have watched TV for forty minutes.
4/117	Chinese	今天下午你想不想看中国的电视?
	English	Do you want to watch Chinese television this afternoon?
5/117	Chinese	我喜欢看电影，不喜欢看电视。
	English	I prefer watching movies to watching television.

是 to be / right / yes shì **118** | **S**

Chinese	English	Character codes
不 + 是 不是	not	007/118
是 + 不是 是不是	whether or not	118/007/118

Example Sentences

1/118	Chinese	他是医生，不是老师。
	English	He is a doctor, not a teacher.
2/118	Chinese	这些书都是我的。
	English	These books are all mine.
3/118	Chinese	今天是不是 6 月 25 号?
	English	Is it the 25th of June today?
4/118	Chinese	她是我的同学。
	English	She is my classmate.
5/118	Chinese	苹果是我很喜欢的水果。
	English	Apples are my favourite fruit.

S | 119　书 book shū

Chinese	English	Character codes
书 + 本 书本	book + measure word for books books	119/006
书 + 店 书店	book + shop bookshop	119/018
汉语 + 书	Chinese + book	038/160/119
买书	buy books	075/119
看书	read books	062/119
读书	study/read books	021/119
一本书	a book	152/006/119

Example Sentences

1/119	Chinese	我有三本汉语书。
	English	I have three Chinese books.
2/119	Chinese	我下午去书店买书。
	English	I will go to the bookshop to buy some books this afternoon.
3/119	Chinese	学校后面有一家很好的中国书店。
	English	There is a good Chinese bookshop behind the school.
4/119	Chinese	A：你想买什么书？ B：我想买一些汉语书。
	English	A: What books do you want to buy? B: I want to buy some Chinese books.
5/119	Chinese	这本书很好，说的都是现在的中国。
	English	This book is very good. It is about modern China.

Chinese	English	Character codes
喝 + 水 喝水	drink +water drink water	041/120
水 + 杯 水杯	water +cup cup	120/004
一 + 杯 + 水 一杯水	a cup of water	152/004/120
水果	water +fruit fruit	120/037
热水	hot +water hot water	103/120
雨水	rain+water rainwater	159/120

Example Sentences

1/120	Chinese	姐姐不喜欢喝热水。
	English	My sister doesn't like hot water.
2/120	Chinese	商店里有很多水果。
	English	There is a lot of fruit in the shop.
3/120	Chinese	那是你的水杯吗?
	English	Is that your cup?
4/120	Chinese	医生叫我多喝水。
	English	The doctor told me to drink more water.
5/120	Chinese	今年雨水太多了。
	English	We've had too much rain this year.

S | 121 睡 sleep shuì

Chinese	English	Character codes
睡 + 觉 睡觉	sleep + sleep sleep	121/056
去 + 睡觉 去睡觉	go to bed	102/121/056
睡 + 午 + 觉 睡午觉	take a nap	121/134/056
睡了一觉	sleep for a while	121/067/152/056
睡了一大觉	sleep for a long time	121/067/152/014/056

Example Sentences

1/121	Chinese	我天天十点睡觉。
	English	I go to bed at ten in the evening each day.
2/121	Chinese	我去睡觉了，好吗?
	English	I am going to sleep, OK?
3/121	Chinese	你中午睡午觉吗?
	English	Do you nap at noon?
4/121	Chinese	我一觉睡了十二个钟点。
	English	I slept for twelve hours straight.
5/121	Chinese	你晚上几点睡觉?
	English	What time do you go to bed at night?

Chinese	English	Character codes
说 + 不 说不	say + no	122/007
不 + 说 不说	don't + say	007/122
说 + 出 说出	speak + out	122/012
说好了	say + good + grammatical code 'le' to make a deal	122/039/067
说话	speak + words speak	122/046
说了话	said	122/067/046
没说	did not say	078/122
说明	speak + bright explain	122/083
能说	can + speak can speak	088/122
你说	you + say you say	089/122
说起	speak+rise talk about	122/097
请说	please+speak say it please	101/122
说什么	speak +what say what	122/111/077
听说	listen + speak hear of/about	129/122
小说	small+speak novel	143/122
怎么说	how to say	165/077/122
说说	speak/tell/explain	122/122

Example Sentences

1/122	Chinese	你说什么？
	English	What did you say?
2/122	Chinese	"Novel" 汉语怎么说？能说说吗？
	English	How do you say 'novel' in Chinese? Can you say it?
3/122	Chinese	他一天都没说话。
	English	He didn't say anything for the whole day.
4/122	Chinese	她昨天在大学说了很多话。
	English	She talked a lot at university yesterday.
5/122	Chinese	我们前天下午说好了我们一起去看这个电影。
	English	The day before yesterday in the afternoon, we agreed we'd see the film together.

S | 123 四 four sì

Chinese	English	Character codes
四＋杯 四杯	four + cup four cups	123/004
四＋本 四本	four + measure word four books	123/006
四＋点 四点 *	four + point four o'clock	123/016
四个	four + four measure word	123/031
四家	four + measure word four (families or companies)	123/053
四个月	four months	123/031/162
四块……	four + measure word four pieces	123/064
四年	four + year four years	123/090
四十	four + ten forty	123/114
四岁	four + year four years old	123/124
四天	four + day four days	123/128
四月	four + month April	123/162

注释 Note

* We can also put a noun after 四点 when 点 means pieces/points and is used as a measure word. For example, we can say 四点意见 which means four suggestions.

Example Sentences

1/123	Chinese	现在是下午四点。
	English	It's currently four o'clock in the afternoon.
2/123	Chinese	他今天喝了四杯水。
	English	He drank four cups of water today.
3/123	Chinese	这杯茶四块钱。
	English	This cup of tea costs four *yuan*.
4/123	Chinese	学校后面有四家商店。
	English	There are four stores behind the school.
5/123	Chinese	他四月回他东北的家，看他的爸爸妈妈。
	English	In April, he will return to his home in the Northeast to visit his dad and mum.

岁 year/age suì 124 | S

Chinese	English	Character codes
八 + 岁 八岁	eight + year eight years old	002/124
几 + 岁 几岁	how many + year how old...	052/124
九 + 岁 九岁	nine + year nine years old	060/124
六岁	six + year six years old	072/124
七岁	seven + year seven years old	095/124
三岁	three + year three years old	106/124
十岁	ten + year ten years old	114/124
四十多岁	four + ten+ more + years in one's forties	123/114/023/124
同岁	same+ year the same age	130/124
年年岁岁	year after year	090/090/124/124

注释　Note

* In the expression 一岁, the pronunciation of 一（first tone）should change to the second tone.
We can only use the question 你几岁了？ when addressing children. It is not polite to use this expression for asking the age of old people.

Example Sentences

1/124	Chinese	你几岁了？ *
	English	How old are you?
2/124	Chinese	他的女儿今年八岁。
	English	His daughter is eight years old.
3/124	Chinese	我和他的姐姐同岁。
	English	I am the same age as his elder sister.
4/124	Chinese	一岁的孩子不能吃米饭。
	English	A one-year-old child is not able to eat rice.
5/124	Chinese	他四十多岁，是北京一个中学的汉语老师。
	English	He's in his forties and is a Chinese teacher in a middle school in Beijing.

T | 125 he/him 他 tā

Chinese	English	Character codes
他 + 爱 他爱……	he + love he loves…	125/001
他 + 吃 他吃……	he + eat he eats…	125/011
他 + 打 他打……	he + hit he hits…	125/013
打他	hit + he hit him	013/125
他的	he + grammatical code his	125/015
他国 *	he+country other country	125/036
他会……	he + know how to he knows how to…	125/049
他喝……	he + drink he drinks…	125/041
他来了	he+ come + grammatical code here he comes	125/065/067
他们	he + suffix for plural they	125/079
他人 *	he + person other people	125/104
他是	he + is he is…	125/118
他想……	he + want he wants…	125/142
他有……	he + has he has…	125/158

注释 Note

* We usually use 他人，他国 in written Chinese.

Example Sentences

1/125	Chinese	他爱读书。
	English	He loves reading.
2/125	Chinese	他有一个很会做中国菜的姐姐。
	English	He has an elder sister who knows how to make Chinese dishes very well.
3/125	Chinese	那个茶杯是他的。
	English	That teacup is his.
4/125	Chinese	他想坐出租车去学校。
	English	He wants to take a taxi to school.
5/125	Chinese	他来我们家的那天，我们家里的狗和猫都很高兴。
	English	The day he came to our home, our dog and cat were very happy.

Chinese	English	Character codes
她 + 爱 她爱……	she + love she loves…	126/001
她 + 吃 她吃……	she + eat she eats…	126/011
她 + 打 她打……	she + hit she hits…	126/013
打她	hit + her hit her	013/126
她的	she + grammatical code her	126/015
她做……	she + do she does…	126/178
她喝……	she + drink she drinks…	126/041
她来了	She + come + grammatical code here she comes	126/065/067
她老了	she+ come+ grammatical code she became old	126/066/067
她们	she + suffix for plural they	126/079
她是	she + is she is…	126/118
她想……	she + wants she wants…	126/142
她有……	she + has she has…	126/158

Example Sentences

1/125	Chinese	她爱吃北京菜。
	English	She likes to eat Beijing food.
2/125	Chinese	她的爸爸是老师。
	English	Her father is a teacher.
3/125	Chinese	她和她们不认识。
	English	She doesn't know them.
4/125	Chinese	我是十年以前认识她的，现在她老了。
	English	I met her ten years ago. Now she is old.
5/125	Chinese	她现在不在家，她出去买菜了。
	English	She is not at home right now. She went out to buy vegetables.

T | 127 太 too / extreme tài

Chinese	English	Character codes
太 + 爱 + 她 太爱她	too + love +her love her so much	127/001/126
不 + 太 不太……	not + too not too...	007/127
吃 + 了 + 太 + 多 吃了太多	eat + grammatical code + too + much ate too much	011/067/127/023
太大(了)	too + big + (grammatical code) too + big	127/014/(067)
太对了	too + correct+ grammatical code absolutely right	127/022/067
太多(了)	too + much + (grammatical code) too much	127/023/(067)
太高(了)	too + high + (grammatical code) too high	127/030/(067)
太好了	too + good + grammatical code great	127/039/067
太后	too + behind queen mother	127/044
火太大了	fire + too + big + grammatical code the fire was too fierce	050/127/014/067
太老了	too + old + grammatical code too old	127/066/067
太冷了	too + cold + grammatical code too cold	127/068/067
太亮了	too + bright + grammatical code too bright	127/070/067
太漂亮了	too + clean + bright + grammatical code so beautiful	127/093/070/067
太气人了	too + anger + person + grammatical code It's too annoying.	127/098/104/067
太热了	too + hot + grammatical code too hot	127/103/067
太少了	too + few + grammatical code too little	127/109/067

续表

Chinese	English	Character codes
太喜欢了	too + happy +joyous + grammatical code love so much	127/137/047/067
太小了	too + small + grammatical code too small	127/143/067
太谢谢了	too + thank + thank + grammatical code thank you so much	127/147/147/067
太太 *	Mrs/madame/wife	127/127
老太太 *	old woman	066/127/127

注释　Note

* 太太 tàitai=Mrs; madame

Example Sentences

1/127	Chinese	我昨天吃太多了，今天不吃了。	
	English	I ate too much yesterday, so I won't eat anything today.	
2/127	Chinese	这儿太冷了，我不喜欢。	
	English	It's too cold here. I don't like it.	
3/127	Chinese	这衣服太漂亮了。	
	English	This dress is so beautiful.	
4/127	Chinese	那个老太太 * 是西北来的，她说的北京话不太好。	
	English	That old woman comes from the Northwest. She can't speak Beijing dialect well.	
5/127	Chinese	雨太大了，不能出去。	
	English	The rain is too heavy. We can't go out.	

T | 128　天 sky/heaven/day tiān

Chinese	English	Character codes
天 + 分 天分	Heaven + divide talent	128/028
天 + 国 天国	sky + country paradise	128/036
天 + 气 天气	sky + air weather	128/098
后天	later + day the day after tomorrow	044/128
几天	how many + day how many days	052/128
今天	today + day today	058/128
老天	old + sky God	066/128
天冷了	sky + cold + grammatical code it is getting cold	128/068/067
天亮了	sky + bright + grammatical code day is breaking	128/070/067
六天	six + day six days	072/128
明天	bright + day tomorrow	083/128
那天	that + day that day	085/128
哪一天	which + one + day which day	084/152/128
天气	sky + air weather	128/098
大热天	big + hot + day very hot day	014/103/128
天天	day + day everyday	128/128
天下	sky + below world	128/139

注释　Note

* 天书 refers to a book that is very difficult to understand.

Example Sentences

1/128	Chinese	明天是个好天气。
	English	It'll be a nice day tomorrow.
2/128	Chinese	你是哪一天生的?
	English	Which day is your birthday?
3/128	Chinese	后天是个大热天。
	English	The day after tomorrow is a hot day.
4/128	Chinese	他天天都回家做饭。
	English	He goes home to cook every day.
5/128	Chinese	这本书和天书 * 一样，我读不了。
	English	This book is like Greek to me. I can't read it.

听 listen/obey tīng 129 | T

Chinese	English	Character codes
不 + 听 + 话 不听话	not + listen + words intractable	007/129/046
听 + 出 + 来 听出来	listen + exit + come distinguish	129/012/065
听 + 多 + 了 听多了	listen + much + grammatical code hear too much	129/023/067
好听	good + listen pleasant to hear	039/129
听候	listen + wait wait for	129/045
听话	listen + words obedient	129/046
听见	listen + see hear	129/054
听了	listen + grammatical code listen	129/067
没听见	not + listen + see didn't hear	078/129/054
视听	vision + listen audio-visual	117/129

Example Sentences

1/129	Chinese	这个女生很不听话。
	English	This female student is not obedient at all.
2/129	Chinese	我在听他说话呢。
	English	I am listening to him right now.
3/129	Chinese	她说话很好听，我很喜欢听。
	English	She has a nice speaking voice. I like to listen very much.
4/129	Chinese	这些话我听多了。
	English	I've heard enough about this.
5/129	Chinese	我没听见他说什么。
	English	I didn't hear what he said.

T | 130　同　same/together　tóng

Chinese	English	Character codes
不 + 同 不同	not + same different	007/130
同 + 名 同名	same + name same name	130/082
同 + 年 同年	same + year same year	130/090
同期	same + period same period	130/096
同时	same + time at the same time	130/115
同岁	same + age the same age	130/124
同一天	same + one + day on the same day	130/152/128
同学	same + study classmate	130/150
同样	same + shape the same	130/151
同住	same + live live together	130/170
同租	same + rent rent together	130/174

注释　Note

* 爱好（hǎo）is a noun and the tone of 好 should be in the fourth.

Example Sentences

1/130	Chinese	我和她爱好 * 不同。	
	English	My hobbies are different from hers.	
2/130	Chinese	他们是同学。	
	English	They are classmates.	
3/130	Chinese	我和他同时打开了汉字书。	
	English	He and I opened the the book of Chinese characters at the same time.	
4/130	Chinese	她和我大姐同岁。	
	English	She is the same age as my eldest sister.	
5/130	Chinese	我们说好了同一天回家。	
	English	We have agreed to go home on the same day.	

Chinese	English	Character codes
喂	hello	131

Example Sentences

1/131	Chinese	喂，你好！
	English	Hello!
2/131	Chinese	喂，高先生在家吗?
	English	Hello, is Mr Gao home?
3/131	Chinese	喂，有人吗?
	English	Hello, is anybody there?
4/131	Chinese	妈妈在喂小女儿吃饭。
	English	The mother is feeding her little daughter.
5/131	Chinese	喂 *，你不能这么做。
	English	Hey, you can't do this.

> 注释 Note
>
> * 喂 can be used to attract attention, like saying 'hey!' Note that 喂 uses the fourth tone here.

W | 132 我 I/me wǒ

Chinese	English	Character codes
我 + 们 我们	we; us	132/079
我 + 爱 +…… 我爱……	I + love I love…	132/001
我 + 爸 + 爸 我爸爸	I + father my father	132/003/003
我吃……	I + eat I eat…	132/011
我打……	I + hit I hit…	132/013
打我	hit + me hit me	013/132
我的	I + grammatical code my; mine	132/015
我会……	I + know how to I can…	132/049
我喝……	I + drink I drink…	132/041
我来了	I + come + grammatical code here I am	132/065/067
我老了	I + come + grammatical code I am old	132/066/067
我生气了	I + produce + anger I am angry	132/112/098/067
我是	I + is I am …	132/118
我想有……	I + want+have I want to have…	132/142/158
我学习……	I + study +review I + study	132/150/136

Example Sentences

1/132	Chinese	我爱我爸爸。
	English	I love my dad.
2/132	Chinese	今天我吃了好吃的中国菜。
	English	Today I had delicious Chinese food.
3/132	Chinese	我想有个漂亮的女朋友。
	English	I want a beautiful girlfriend.
4/132	Chinese	明年我想在北京学习汉语。
	English	I'd like to study Chinese in Beijing next year.
5/132	Chinese	我生气了，不想再见他了。
	English	I am angry and don't want to see him anymore.

W | 133　五 five wǔ

Chinese	English	Character codes
五 + 杯 五杯	five + cup five cups	133/004
五 + 本 五本	five + measure word for books five books	133/006
五 + 点 五点	five + point five o'clock	133/016
五个	five + measure word five (pieces, exc)	133/031
五家	five + measure word five (families or companies)	133/053
五姐	five + older sister fifth-born sister	133/057
五 + 块 五块（钱）	five + measure word five yuan	133/064/(100)
五年	five + year five years	133/090
五十	five + ten fifty	133/114
五岁	five + year of age five years old	133/124
五天	five + day five days	133/128
五月	five + month May	133/162
五个月	five + MW + month five months	133/031/162

Example Sentences

1/133	Chinese	他五点回去做饭。
	English	He goes back to cook at five o'clock.
2/133	Chinese	他今天去了五家商店。
	English	He went to five stores today.
3/133	Chinese	今年五月天气很好。
	English	This year the weather has been very good in May.
4/133	Chinese	我认识他五年了，那时候他是个北京的学生。
	English	I've known him for five years. During that time, he has been a student in Beijing.
5/133	Chinese	我有五本很好的汉语书，那是我去年在北京一家很小的书店买的。
	English	I have five good Chinese books that I bought from a small bookshop in Beijing last year.

午 noon/the middle of the day wǔ 134 | W

Chinese	English	Character codes
午 + 后 午后	the middle of the day + behind afternoon	134/044
上 + 午 上午	above + the middle of the day morning	108/134
午 + 时 午时	the middle of day + time noon	134/115
午睡	the middle of the day + sleep nap; siesta	134/121
下午	below + the middle of the day afternoon	139/134
中午	middle + the middle of the day noon	168/134

Example Sentences

1/134	Chinese	他天天上午都学习。
	English	Every day, he studies in the morning.
2/134	Chinese	我中午都会午睡。
	English	I take a nap every noon.
3/134	Chinese	午后天气很热。
	English	It's very hot in the afternoon.
4/134	Chinese	我们下午去电影院看电影好吗？
	English	Shall we go to the cinema in the afternoon?
5/134	Chinese	他是昨天中午的时候回来的。
	English	He came back at lunchtime yesterday.

X | 135　西　west xī

Chinese	English	Character codes
西 + 北 西北	west + north northwest	135/005
东 + 西 东西	east + west thing	019/135
西 + 面 西面	west + side west side	135/081
在西面	at+ west + side on the western side	164/135/081
西医	west + doctor Western medicine	135/154

Example Sentences

1/135	Chinese	他家在中国的西北。	
	English	His family is in Northwest China.	
2/135	Chinese	这是什么东西？	
	English	What's this?	
3/135	Chinese	医院在商店西面。	
	English	The hospital is to the west of the store.	
4/135	Chinese	学校的西面是一家很好的电影院。	
	English	To the west of the school is a very good cinema.	
5/135	Chinese	这家饭店的东面和西面都是水果店，那儿什么水果都有。	
	English	To both the west and east of this hotel there are fruit shops. There you can find every type of fruit.	

习 practise/review/be used to/habit xí **136** **X**

Chinese	English	Character codes
习 + 气 习气	practice + air bad habit	136/098
学 + 习 学习	study + review study	150/136

Example Sentences

1/136	Chinese	他是个爱学习的好学生。
	English	He is a good student who loves learning.
2/136	Chinese	我在学习汉语呢！
	English	I'm studying Chinese.
3/136	Chinese	我喜欢在学校读书学习。
	English	I like reading and studying at school.
4/136	Chinese	我们都有一些不好的习气。
	English	We all have some bad habits.
5/136	Chinese	小明家里没有钱，他一面在饭馆工作一面在学校学习。
	English	Little Ming's family has no money, so he works in a restaurant alongside his study at school.

X | 137 喜 happy/be fond of xǐ

Chinese	English	Character codes
喜 + 爱 喜爱	be fond of + love love	137/001
喜 + 欢 喜欢	be fond of + joyous like	137/047
不 + 喜 + 欢 不喜欢	not + be fond of + joyous don't like	007/137/047
喜气	happy + air festivity	137/098
同喜	same + happy share happiness	130/137
欢欢喜喜	joyous and happy	047/047/137/137
大喜	big + happy great happiness	014/137

Example Sentences

1/137	Chinese	我喜爱喝茶。	
	English	I like drinking tea.	
2/137	Chinese	他喜欢的是那个女生。	
	English	What he likes is that female student.	
3/137	Chinese	我们都不喜欢很热的天气。	
	English	Neither of us like hot weather.	
4/137	Chinese	我听说你有了一个儿子，大喜大喜！	
	English	I heard you now have a son, congratulations!	
5/137	Chinese	这衣服看起来很喜气。	
	English	This outfit looks very festive.	

系 link / tie / series / department / system xì 138 X

Chinese	English	Character codes
关 + 系 关系	close + link relation	034/138
水 + 系 水系	water + link river system	120/138
星 + 系 星系	star + link galaxy	148/138
院系	college + department department	161/138

Example Sentences

1/138	Chinese	我们的关系很好。
	English	We get along well with each other.
2/138	Chinese	在我们大学，同学关系都很好。
	English	At our university, the relationship among our classmates is very good.
3/138	Chinese	你是哪个院系的?
	English	Which department of the university are you from?
4/138	Chinese	我想认识不同的星系。
	English	I'd like to find out a little about a different galaxy.
5/138	Chinese	在大学的时候，我读的是汉学系。
	English	When I was at university, I studied sinology.

X | 139　下　below / down / next / come down　xià

Chinese	English	Character codes
下 + 面 下面	below + side below	139/081
桌子 + 下面 桌子下面	under the table	171/172/139/081
下 + 午 下午	below + the middle of the day afternoon	139/134
天下	sky + below world	128/139
下飞机	get off the flight	139/027/051
下个月	next month	139/031/162
下雨	down + rain rain	139/159
下一站	down+one+station next station	139/152/166

Example Sentences

1/139	Chinese	他下个月回来。	
	English	He will come back next month.	
2/139	Chinese	我下飞机后去见你。	
	English	I'll visit you when I get off the plane.	
3/139	Chinese	桌子下面是椅子。	
	English	There are chairs under the table.	
4/139	Chinese	下雨了，他不能来了。	
	English	It's raining, so he can't come now.	
5/139	Chinese	这一站不是，我在下一站下车。	
	English	This isn't the stop I want. I will get off at the next one.	

先 earlier / first / older generation / ahead / before xiān **140** | **X**

Chinese	English	Character codes
先 + 吃 先吃	earlier + eat eat first	140/011
先 + 出 + 去 先出去	earlier + exit + go go out first	140/012/102
先 + 生 先生	first + man sir; Mr	140/112
先前	first + before before	140/099
先后	first + behind one after the other	140/044
先说	earlier + speak speak first	140/122

Example Sentences

1/140	Chinese	谢先生你先吃。
	English	Mr Xie, you eat first.
2/140	Chinese	先生，电影院在哪儿?
	English	Sir, where is the cinema?
3/140	Chinese	我先出去一下。
	English	I'll be out for a moment.
4/140	Chinese	我先前不认识这个人。
	English	I didn't know this person before.
5/140	Chinese	今天我和我的同学在中国饭馆吃饭，一点的时候，大家先后都来了。
	English	Today, my classmates and I had a meal in a Chinese restaurant. At one o'clock, everyone arrived one after the other.

X | 141 现 now/present/show/appear xiàn

Chinese	English	Character codes
现 + 今 现今	now + today nowadays	141/058
现 + 有 现有	now + have existing	141/158
现 + 在 现在	now + at now	141/164
现做	now + make freshly made	141/178
现钱	now + money cash	141/100
出现	exit + appear appear	012/141

Example Sentences

1/141	Chinese	现在我不能睡觉。	
	English	I can't sleep now.	
2/141	Chinese	他现在住在学校里。	
	English	He currently lives on campus.	
3/141	Chinese	这些菜是现做的。	
	English	This food was made just now.	
4/141	Chinese	先生，您有现钱吗?	
	English	Sir, do you have cash?	
5/141	Chinese	谢医生几天没有出现了，有人说，他去北京了。	
	English	Dr Xie hasn't turned up for a few days. Some people said he had gone to Beijing.	

Chinese	English	Character codes
想 + 吃 想吃	want + eat want to eat	142/011
想 + 读 想读	want + read want to read	142/021
好 + 想 好想	good + want really want	039/142
很想	very + want really want	043/142
想回家	want + go back + home want to go back home	142/048/053
想见	want + see want to see	142/054
想买	want + buy want to buy	142/075
想起来	want + rise + come remember	142/097/065
想认识	want + know + recognise want to know	142/105/116

Example Sentences

1/142	Chinese	我想吃一些水果。
	English	I want to eat some fruit.
2/142	Chinese	我很想回家。
	English	I really want to go back home.
3/142	Chinese	他想认识那个漂亮的女生。
	English	He wants to get to know that beautiful girl.
4/142	Chinese	他们很想开车去学校。
	English	They really want to drive to school.
5/142	Chinese	我现在脑子不好，想不起来她昨天说的话了。
	English	My memory is so poor now. I can't remember what she said yesterday.

X | 143 小 small / young / little / lovely xiǎo

Chinese	English	Character codes
小 + 菜 小菜	little + dish side dishes	143/008
小 + 店 小店	little + store small store	143/018
小 + 狗 小狗	little + dog little dog	143/033
小姐	little + sister Miss	143/057
小猫	little + cat little cat	143/076
小雨	little + rain light rain/drizzle	143/159
小桌子	little + desk + suffix small desk	143/171/172

Example Sentences

1/143	Chinese	这是一家小店。
	English	This is a small shop.
2/143	Chinese	我喜欢米老师家的小桌子。
	English	I like the small desk in Teacher Mi's home.
3/143	Chinese	那个很高的女生是国小姐。
	English	That tall female student is Miss Guo.
4/143	Chinese	今天和明天的天气都很好，后天有小雨。
	English	Today and tomorrow the weather will be good. The day after tomorrow, there will be light rain.
5/143	Chinese	请上几个小菜和一杯茶。你们有没有面？我很想吃点儿面。
	English	Please give us some side dishes and a cup of tea. Do you serve noodles? I really want to eat some noodles.

校 school xiào 144 | X

Chinese	English	Character codes
高 + 校 高校	high + school university	030/144
学 + 校 学校	study + school school	150/144
校 + 医 + 院 校医院	school+ medicine + yard school infirmary	144/154/161
住校	live + school live on campus	170/144
同校	same+ school in the same school	130/144

Example Sentences

1/144	Chinese	她去学校了。	
	English	She went to school.	
2/144	Chinese	他们九月回学校。	
	English	They go back to school in September.	
3/144	Chinese	他在校医院工作。	
	English	He works in the school infirmary.	
4/144	Chinese	中国有很多不同的高校。	
	English	There are many different kinds of universities in China.	
5/144	Chinese	现在中国人有钱了，很多学校的学生都是住校生。	
	English	Now that Chinese people are richer, many students live on campus.	

X | 145 些 some xiē

Chinese	English	Character codes
多 + 些 多些	many + some more	023/145
高 + 些 高些	tall + some taller	030/145
好 + 些 好些（了）	good + some getting better	039/145/(067)
老些（了）	old + some older	066/145/(067)
冷些（了）	cold + some colder	068/145/(067)
少些	less + some less	109/145
一些	one + some some	152/145

Example Sentences

1/145	Chinese	我有一些水果，你吃吗？
	English	I have some fruit. Would you like to eat some?
2/145	Chinese	今天天气冷些了。
	English	Today it is colder.
3/145	Chinese	我和我姐姐十年没有见面了，她老了些。
	English	My elder sister and I haven't seen each other for 10 years. She is older now.
4/145	Chinese	今天的菜多些。
	English	There are more dishes today.
5/145	Chinese	喝了热水，我好些了。
	English	After drinking hot water, I feel a bit better.

写 write/compose xiě 146 | X

Chinese	English	Character codes
不 + 写 不写	no + write don't write	007/146
写 + 出 写出	write + out write out	146/012
写 + 对 写对	write + right write correctly	146/022
写了个字	write a character	146/067/031/173
写好了	has already written	146/039/067
没写	didn't + write didn't write	078/146
写字	write + character write characters	146/173
在桌子上写	on + table + up+ write write on the table	164/171/172/108/146

Example Sentences

1/146	Chinese	他不爱写汉字。	
	English	He does not like to write Chinese characters.	
2/146	Chinese	小明说他今天一个字都没有写。	
	English	Little Ming says that he didn't write a word today.	
3/146	Chinese	这些汉字他们都写好了。	
	English	They have written all of those characters.	
4/146	Chinese	大家都写对了那个字。	
	English	Everyone wrote that character correctly.	
5/146	Chinese	他在桌子上写了三个字。	
	English	He wrote three characters on the table.	

X | 147　谢 thank / a family name　xiè

Chinese	English	Character codes
不 + 谢 不谢	no + thank not at all	007/147
谢 + 谢 谢谢	thank + thank thanks	147/147
说 + 谢谢 说谢谢	say thanks	122/147
谢谢你	thank + thank+ you thank you	147/147/089

Example Sentences

1/147	Chinese	谢谢你对我这么好。
	English	Thanks for treating me so kindly.
2/147	Chinese	谢谢大家的关爱。
	English	Thank you all for your care.
3/147	Chinese	谢谢你的苹果。
	English	Thank you for the apples.
4/147	Chinese	不谢，不客气，我们是朋友。
	English	Don't mention it, it's nothing. We are friends.
5/147	Chinese	我们是好同学，是多年的好朋友，不说谢。
	English	We are good classmates and have been good friends for many years, so there is no need to say thanks.

Chinese	English	Character codes
星 + 星 + 点 + 点 星星点点	bit + bit + point + point bits and pieces	148/148/016/016
星 + 火 星火	bit + fire spark	148/050
火 + 星 火星	fire + star Mars	050/148
明星	bright + star star; celebrity	083/148
女星	female + star female star	091/148
星期	star + period week	148/096
水星	water + star Mercury	120/148
星星	star + star stars	148/148

Example Sentences

1/148	Chinese	我们星期一去学校。	
	English	We go to school on Monday.	
2/148	Chinese	大家星期天都不工作。	
	English	People don't work on Sundays.	
3/148	Chinese	下个星期我去中国。	
	English	I'll go to China next week.	
4/148	Chinese	天上的星星很亮。	
	English	The stars in the sky are bright.	
5/148	Chinese	我昨天看了一个电影，里面的那个女星很漂亮。	
	English	I watched a film yesterday. An actress in that movie is very pretty.	

X | 149 兴 exciting / interest xìng

Chinese	English	Character codes
高 + 兴 高兴	high+excited glad; happy	30/149
很 + 高 + 兴 很高兴	very happy	043/030/149
有 + 点 + 高兴 有点高兴	a little happy	158/016/030/149
有点不高兴	a bit unhappy	158/016/007/030/149
不高兴	unhappy	007/030/149
很高兴	very happy	043/030/149
太高兴了	so happy	127/030/149/067
不太高兴	not very happy	007/127/030/149

Example Sentences

1/149	Chinese	这几天爸爸妈妈都很高兴。	
	English	Father and mother have been very happy over the last few days.	
2/149	Chinese	妈妈有点儿不高兴。	
	English	Mum is a bit unhappy.	
3/149	Chinese	我今天太高兴了。	
	English	I am so happy today.	
4/149	Chinese	今天高老师怎么了，是不是不太高兴？	
	English	What happened to Teacher Gao today? Is she a bit upset?	
5/149	Chinese	你什么时候会不高兴？	
	English	When are you unhappy?	

学 study/imitate xué **150** | **X**

Chinese	English	Character codes
学 + 校 学校	school	150/144
爱 + 学 爱学	love + study love to study	001/150
学 + 习 学习	learn	150/136
爱学习	love to learn	001/150/136
不学	not learn	007/150
学车	study+car learn to drive	150/010
大学	university	014/150
学分	credit	150/028
汉学	sinology	038/150
好学	fond of+study studious	039/150
学会	study+know how to master	150/049
开学	school starts	061/150
学年	academic year	150/090
学期	term	150/096
学前	study+ in advance pre-school	150/099
上学	go to school	108/150
学生	student	150/112
同学	classmates; fellow students	130/150
西学	west+study Western learning	135/150
小学	primary school	143/150
医学	medical science	154/150
学院	college	150/161

Example Sentences

1/150	Chinese	我很爱学习，很喜欢医学。	
	English	I love to study and really like medical science.	
2/150	Chinese	现在我在上大学。	
	English	I'm currently studying at university.	
3/150	Chinese	你喜欢汉学吗?	
	English	Do you like sinology?	
4/150	Chinese	开学后你想做什么?	
	English	What do you want to do after school starts?	
5/150	Chinese	我现在学会做这个中国菜了。	
	English	I have learned how to cook this Chinese dish.	

Y | 151 样 shape/appearance/model yàng

Chinese	English	Character codes
小 + 样 小样	sample	143/151
一 + 样 一样	same	152/151
样 + 子 样子	appearance	151/172
不一样	not+one+kind different	007/152/151
样本	appearance +original sample	151/006

Example Sentences

1/151	Chinese	爸爸和妈妈一样爱我。
	English	Dad and mum love me the same.
2/151	Chinese	医学和汉学不一样。
	English	Medicine and sinology are not the same.
3/151	Chinese	你高兴的时候是什么样子的?
	English	When you are happy, what do you look like?
4/151	Chinese	你想用这些小样吗?
	English	Would you like to use these samples?
5/151	Chinese	你能说说大学和中学有什么不一样吗?
	English	Are you able to explain the differences between the university and the secondary school?

一 one / single / same yī **152** **Y**

Chinese	English	Character codes
一 + 本 + 书 一本书	one+measure word+book a book	152/006/119
一 + 点 + 儿 一点儿	a little	152/016/024
一 + 会 + 儿 一会儿	a moment	152/049/024
一分钟	one minute	152/028/169
一个	one+measure word a single unit of	152/031
一块	a piece of	152/064
一岁	one year old	152/124
一些	some	152/145

Example Sentences

1/152	Chinese	爸爸买了一本书。
	English	My father bought a book.
2/152	Chinese	爸爸大妈妈一岁。
	English	Father is one year older than Mother.
3/152	Chinese	你先去，我一会儿再去。
	English	You go first. I'll go a bit later.
4/152	Chinese	今天有一点儿热。
	English	It's a bit hot today.
5/152	Chinese	我明天去看大学的几个老师，我想多买一些苹果。
	English	Tomorrow I will visit some university teachers, so I want to buy more apples.

Y | 153 衣 clothes yī

Chinese	English	Character codes
大 + 衣 大衣	overcoat	014/153
衣 + 服 衣服	clothes	153/029
衣服 + 店 衣服店	clothing shop	153/029/018
开衣服店	open a clothing shop	061/153/029/018
上衣	top + clothes coat; shirt	108/153

Example Sentences

1/153	Chinese	我很喜欢这个大衣。
	English	I like this overcoat very much.
2/153	Chinese	我昨天去衣服店了。
	English	I went to the clothing shop yesterday.
3/153	Chinese	妈妈想开衣服店。
	English	Mother wants to open a clothing shop.
4/153	Chinese	这是我昨天在一家北京衣服店买的上衣，怎么样，漂亮吗?
	English	This is the shirt I bought yesterday at a Beijing clothing shop. What do you think? Is it beautiful?
5/153	Chinese	我上个星期听高医生说，你很会做衣服，是吗?
	English	Last week I heard Doctor Gao said you were adept at making clothes. Is that true?

医 medicine/cure/treat yī **154** | **Y**

Chinese	English	Character codes
医 + 生 医生	doctor	154/112
医 + 学 医学	medicine + knowledge medicine	154/150
名 + 医 名医	famous + doctor famous doctor	82/154
女医生	female + doctor female doctor	91/154/112
医师	medicine + master physician	154/113
西医	western + medicine Western medicine	135/154
医院	cure + place hospital	154/161
中医	Chinese + medicine traditional Chinese medicine	168/154
医书	medical books	154/119

Example Sentences

1/154	Chinese	车老师的爸爸妈妈都是医生。
	English	Teacher Che's mother and father are both doctors.
2/154	Chinese	我的老师是一个好医生，不是名医。
	English	My teacher is a good doctor, but not a famous one.
3/154	Chinese	我明天开车去那家工人医院。
	English	Tomorrow I will drive to the Worker's Hospital.
4/154	Chinese	中医和西医，你喜欢哪个?
	English	Given Chinese medicine and Western medicine, which one do you prefer?
5/154	Chinese	我的汉语老师说中医很好，我想看看中医的书，你有没有?
	English	My Chinese teacher said that Chinese medicine is very good, so I would like to read some books on Chinese medicine. Do you have any?

Y | 155　椅　chair　yǐ

Chinese	English	Character codes
椅 + 子 椅子	chair+surffix chair	155/172
高 + 椅子 高椅子	tall + chair high chairs	030/155/172
买 + 椅子 买椅子	buy a chair	075/155/172
桌椅	table + chair table and chair	171/155

Example Sentences

1/155	Chinese	老师坐在椅子上看书。
	English	The teacher is sitting on the chair reading a book.
2/155	Chinese	我喜欢在椅子上睡觉。
	English	I like to sleep on chairs.
3/155	Chinese	明天你去不去买椅子？
	English	Will you go to buy a chair tomorrow?
4/155	Chinese	我们学校这个学期买了很多桌椅。
	English	This term our school bought a lot of tables and chairs.
5/155	Chinese	妈妈坐在椅子上一面喝茶一面看书。
	English	Mother is sitting on a chair, drinking tea and reading a book.

影 shadow/film yǐng **156** | **Y**

Chinese	English	Character codes
影 + 子 影子	shadow	156/172
电 + 影 电影	film	017/156
人 + 影 人影	person+shadow figure	104/156

Example Sentences

1/156	Chinese	我什么电影都爱看。
	English	I love to watch all kinds of movies.
2/156	Chinese	高老师和谢医生说他们开车去看电影。
	English	Teacher Gao and Doctor Xie said they will drive to the cinema to watch a movie.
3/156	Chinese	你喜欢什么样的电影?
	English	What kind of movies do you like?
4/156	Chinese	你是什么时候去看电影的?
	English	When did you go to the movie?
5/156	Chinese	姐姐天天都不在家，妈妈很生气，对我说，我们什么时候能看见她的影子?
	English	My elder sister goes out every day, so mother became angry. She said to me, 'When will we be able to see her?'

Y | 157   友 friend yǒu

Chinese	English	Character codes
朋 + 友 朋友	friend + friend friend	092/157
友 + 爱 友爱	friend +love friendly	157/001
好 + 友 好友	good friend	039/157
女友	girlfriend	091/157

Example Sentences

1/157	Chinese	他们都是我的好友。
	English	All of them are my good friends.
2/157	Chinese	A: 你有多少个中国朋友？ B: 我有很多很多的中国朋友。
	English	A: How many Chinese friends do you have? B: I have a lot of Chinese friends.
3/157	Chinese	我没有女友，你呢？
	English	I do not have a girlfriend, what about you?
4/157	Chinese	我和我朋友想去看一个中国电影，你去不去？
	English	My friend and I are going to see a Chinese film. Would you like to join us?
5/157	Chinese	你有多少朋友在北京？我的朋友都在东北，北京没有几个。
	English	How many friends do you have in Beijing? All my friends are in the Northeast. There are only a few in Beijing.

有 have/exist yǒu 158 | Y

Chinese	English	Character codes
有 + 车 有车	there is a car	158/010
有 + 电 有电	there is electricity	158/017
没 + 有 没有	have not	078/158
有客人	have a guest	158/063/104
有名	famous	158/082
有钱	have + money rich	158/100
有人	someone	158/104
有水	have water	158/120
现有	existing	141/158
有些	some	158/145
想有	want to have	142/158

Example Sentences

1/158	Chinese	你有车吗？	
	English	Do you have a car?	
2/158	Chinese	我不想做一个有钱人，想做一个高高兴兴的人。	
	English	I don't want to be a rich man. I want to be a happy person.	
3/158	Chinese	今天我家里有客人。	
	English	There are guests in my home today.	
4/158	Chinese	小高的朋友有些是大学的同学，有些是中学的同学。	
	English	Some of Little Gao's friends are fellow students from university and others are classmates from high school.	
5/158	Chinese	高老师和米老师都有很多书。	
	English	Teachers Gao and Mi both have a lot of books.	

Y | 159 雨 rain yǔ

Chinese	English	Character codes
下 + 雨 下雨	rain	139/159
下雨 + 天 下雨天	rain + day rainy day	139/159/128
雨 + 点 雨点	raindrop	159/016
雨衣	rain + coat raincoat	159/153
多雨	rainy	023/159
没雨	no rain	078/159
雨水	rain + water rainwater	159/120
大雨	heavy + rain heavy rain	014/159
下大雨	down+heavy+ rain downpour	139/014/159
小雨	light rain	143/159
有雨	have+rain there is rain	158/159

Example Sentences

1/159	Chinese	我喜欢下雨天。
	English	I like rainy days.
2/159	Chinese	现在下大雨了，我没有雨衣，你有吗？
	English	It is raining heavily right now. I don't have a raincoat, do you?
3/159	Chinese	下雨了，你会去医院吗？
	English	It is raining. Will you go to the hospital?
4/159	Chinese	妈妈说：“今天有雨，星期三、六和星期天都有雨。”
	English	Mother said, 'There is rain today. It will also rain on Wednesday, Saturday and Sunday.'
5/159	Chinese	A：明天会不会下大雨？ B：不会，电视上说明天上午有小雨，下午没有雨。
	English	A: Will there be heavy rain tomorrow? B: I don't think so. The television forecast said there will be light rain tomorrow morning but no rain in the afternoon.

Chinese	English	Character codes
国 + 语 国语	national + language national language	036/160
汉 + 语 汉语	Chinese	038/160
话 + 语 话语	speech + language discourse	046/160
习语	habit + language idiom	136/160

Example Sentences

1/160	Chinese	我喜欢学习汉语。
	English	I like learning Chinese.
2/160	Chinese	汉语和国语一样不一样?
	English	Is Putonghua the same as the Chinese language?
3/160	Chinese	你会说汉语吗?
	English	Can you speak Chinese?
4/160	Chinese	我今天很高兴，一天学了 20 个习语。
	English	I was very happy today because I learned twenty idioms.
5/160	Chinese	有些人说汉语不好学，有些人说汉语好学。
	English	Some people say Chinese is hard to study, but others say it is easy to study.

Y | 161 院 campus/courtyard yuǎn

Chinese	English	Character codes
北 + 院 北院	north courtyard	005/161
院 + 子 院子	courtyard	161/172
大 + 院子 大院子	big yard	014/161/172
书院	academy of classical learning	119/161
院校	institution	161/144
学院	college	150/161
医院	hospital	154/161
住院	stay in+courtyard hospitalized	170/161
电影院	cinema	017/156/161

Example Sentences

1/161	Chinese	我家的院子很大。
	English	The courtyard at my house is quite big.
2/161	Chinese	你是什么时候去的医院?
	English	When did you go to the hospital?
3/161	Chinese	这是我的学院，他是学院里的老师。
	English	This is my college. He is a college teacher.
4/161	Chinese	我的老师住院了，我明天去医院看看她。
	English	My teacher was hospitalized. I will visit her in the hospital tomorrow.
5/161	Chinese	我姐姐坐出租车去医院，我开车去。
	English	My elder sister takes a taxi to the hospital. I will drive there.

月 month/moon yuè 162 | Y

Chinese	English	Character codes
月 + 租 月租	month+rent monthly rent	162/174
本 + 月 本月	this month	006/162
八 + 月 八月	August	002/162
九月	September	060/162
月亮	moon	162/070
六月	June	072/162
明月	bright moon	083/162
岁月	years	124/162
这月	this month	167/162

Example Sentences

1/162	Chinese	爸爸妈妈都喜欢看月亮，月亮很漂亮。	
	English	Mum and Dad both like to look at the moon. The moon is very beautiful.	
2/162	Chinese	小高，你看天上，你喜不喜欢今天的月亮？	
	English	Little Gao, look at the sky. Do you like tonight's moon?	
3/162	Chinese	北京的八月热不热？	
	English	Is it hot in Beijing in August or not?	
4/162	Chinese	今天的月亮又大又漂亮。	
	English	The moon today is large and beautiful.	
5/162	Chinese	出租车的月租很高，开出租车的人都说，他们天天都是十二点睡觉，六点出车，一天工作十二个小时。	
	English	The monthly rent for taxis is very high, so taxi drivers all say they have to work for 12 hours a day. They go to bed at midnight and go out to work at six o'clock in the morning.	

Z | 163 再 again/then zài

Chinese	English	Character codes
再 + 会 再会	again+meet see you again	163/049
再 + 来 再来	again+come come again	163/065
再 + 买 再买	again+buy buy again	163/075
再去	go again	163/102
再吃	eat again	163/011
再读	read again	163/021
再叫	call again	163/055
再说	say again; put off until some time	163/122
再听	listen again	163/129
再学	learn again	163/150
再见	goodbye	163/054
再写	write again	163/146
再看	look again	163/062
再三	repeatedly	163/106
再回来	back again	163/048/065
再回学校	go back to school	163/048/150/144

Example Sentences

1/163	Chinese	老师再见!	
	English	Goodbye teacher!	
2/163	Chinese	我会再来的。	
	English	I will come again.	
3/163	Chinese	再读一回怎么样?	
	English	How about reading it again?	
4/163	Chinese	你有雨衣吗? 妈妈再三说今天会下雨。	
	English	Do you have a raincoat? Mum said repeatedly it'd rain today.	
5/163	Chinese	我不去西北, 我想在北京再学一个月的汉语。	
	English	I won't go to the Northwest. I would like to stay in Beijing to study Chinese for another month.	

在 in / at / on / exist / be located zài 164 | Z

Chinese	English	Character codes
坐 + 在 坐在	sit on	177/164
不 + 在 不在	not in	007/164
在 + 医 + 院 在医院	in hospital	164/154/161
在饭店	in the hotel	164/026/018
在工作	be working	164/032/176
在中国	in China	164/168/036
在喝茶	be drinking tea	164/041/009
没在	not here	078/164
在睡觉	be sleeping	164/121/056
在校生	school student	164/144/112
在做	be doing	164/178
在做菜	be cooking	164/178/008

Example Sentences

1/164	Chinese	妈妈在医院工作。	
	English	Mother works in the hospital.	
2/164	Chinese	我爸爸在饭店工作。	
	English	My dad works in the hotel.	
3/164	Chinese	老师在做菜，没在喝茶。	
	English	The teacher is cooking and not drinking tea.	
4/164	Chinese	你想在椅子上睡觉吗？	
	English	Do you want to sleep on a chair?	
5/164	Chinese	大家都在学习汉语，你在做什么呢？	
	English	Everyone is studying Chinese. What are you doing?	

Z | 165 怎 how / what / why zěn

Chinese	English	Character codes
怎么 + 样 怎么样	how about	165/077/151
怎么 + 了 怎么了？	how + grammar code What happened?	165/077/067
没 + 怎么 没怎么	nothing	078/165/077

Example Sentences

1/165	Chinese	这菜是怎么做的？	
	English	How do you make this dish?	
2/165	Chinese	A: 你今天怎么了？ B: 我没怎么，我很好。	
	English	A：What happened to you today? B：Nothing, I'm fine.	
3/165	Chinese	你怎么去医院？	
	English	How will you go to the hospital?	
4/165	Chinese	老师今天怎么这么高兴？	
	English	Why is the teacher so happy today?	
5/165	Chinese	你姐姐昨天住院了，她现在怎么样了？	
	English	Your elder sister was hospitalized yesterday. How is she today?	

站 station/stop/stand zhàn 166 | Z

Chinese	English	Character codes
火 + 车 + 站 火车站	fire+vehicle+station train station	050/010/166
车 + 站 车站	station; stop	010/166
出 + 站 出站	out+station exit a station	012/166
水电站	water+electricity+station hydropower station	120/017/166
哪站	which station	084/166
上一站	previous stop	108/152/166
站住	stand+stay stop; halt	166/170
下一站	the next stop	139/152/166

Example Sentences

1/166	Chinese	我想在下一站下车，你下吗?
	English	I'll get off at the next stop. Will you also get off there?
2/166	Chinese	我天天都去西站坐火车。
	English	Every day I go to the West Railway Station to take a train.
3/166	Chinese	我们是同一站下车。
	English	We get off at the same station.
4/166	Chinese	我坐爸爸开的车去车站。
	English	I go to the station in my dad's car.
5/166	Chinese	北京的西客站是一个很大的火车站，天天都有很多人上下车。
	English	Beijing West Railway Station is very big. Every day many people get on and get off trains there.

Z | 167 这 this / here zhè; zhèi

Chinese	English	Character codes
这 + 杯 这杯	this cup	167/004
这 + 本 + 书 这本书	this+measure word+book this book	167/006/119
这 + 菜 这菜	this dish	167/008
这茶	this tea	167/009
这车	this car	167/010
这个	this one	167/031
这家	this family	167/053
这猫	this cat	167/076
这人	this person	167/104
这儿	this+suffix here	167/024
这里	this+inside here	167/069

Example Sentences

1/167	Chinese	这本书很好看。
	English	This book is interesting.
2/167	Chinese	这车是我爸爸的。
	English	This car belongs to my father.
3/167	Chinese	这菜是妈妈做的。我很喜欢吃。
	English	This dish is made by my mother. I like it very much.
4/167	Chinese	这个饭店里的人都说汉语。
	English	All the staff in this hotel speak Chinese.
5/167	Chinese	我们在这个商店里买桌子，在那个商店里买椅子，怎么样?
	English	Shall we buy a table in this shop and chairs in that shop?

中 middle/in/among/centre zhōng **168** | **Z**

Chinese	English	Character codes
中 + 号 中号	medium+number medium size	168/040
中 + 国 中国	China	168/36
中国 + 菜 中国菜	Chinese dish	168/036/008
中午	noon	168/134
中东	middle+east the Middle East	168/019
高中	high+middle high school	030/168
期中	period+middle half mid-term	096/168
中学	middle+study secondary school	168/150

Example Sentences

1/168	Chinese	你来中国几年了?
	English	How many years have you been in China?
2/168	Chinese	你喜不喜欢中国菜?
	English	Do you like Chinese food?
3/168	Chinese	我很想我的高中朋友。
	English	I really miss my high school friends.
4/168	Chinese	高小姐昨天看中了一个中国的电视机。
	English	Yesterday, Miss Gao took a fancy to a television made in China.
5/168	Chinese	我九月中去中东看看，我大学的一个同学在那儿工作。
	English	In the middle of September, I will go to the Middle East. One of my fellow students from university is working there.

Z | 169 钟 clock/bell zhōng

Chinese	English	Character codes
大 + 钟 大钟	big clock	014/169
钟 + 点 钟点	hour	169/016
分 + 钟 分钟	minute	028/169
买一个钟	buy a clock	075/152/031/169
时钟	time + clock clock	115/169

Example Sentences

1/169	Chinese	我开车去商店买了一个钟。
	English	I drove to the store and bought a clock.
2/169	Chinese	我叫了老师十分钟，他都没听见。
	English	I called my teacher for ten minutes, but he didn't hear me.
3/169	Chinese	饭店里有一个大钟。
	English	There is a large clock in the hotel.
4/169	Chinese	你一分钟能写多少个汉字？
	English	How many Chinese characters can you write in one minute?
5/169	Chinese	我和我的朋友说好了，明天上午九点三十分在大钟那儿见面。
	English	My friend and I have fixed the meeting time at 9.30 a.m. tomorrow near the big clock.

住 reside/live/stay/stop zhù 170 | Z

Chinese	English	Character codes
吃 + 住 吃住	eat and live	011/170
住 + 家 住家	live+family resident	170/053
住 + 在 住在	live+locate live at	170/164
住在中国	live in China	170/164/168/036
同住	live together	130/170
住校	board at school	170/144
住院	hospitalized	170/161

Example Sentences

1/170	Chinese	我住在学校。	
	English	I live at school.	
2/170	Chinese	我女朋友的妈妈住院了，我想去看看她。	
	English	The mother of my girlfriend is hospitalized. I'd like to see her.	
3/170	Chinese	我们四个人同住。	
	English	The four of us live together.	
4/170	Chinese	你喜欢住在家里还是喜欢住在学校？	
	English	Do you like living at home or at school?	
5/170	Chinese	他们的家我和我姐姐不能住了，我们没有钱了，不能再租了。	
	English	My elder sister and I can't live in their home anymore. We don't have any money, so we cannot renew the lease.	

Z | 171 桌 desk/table zhuō

Chinese	English	Character codes
一 + 桌 + 菜 一桌菜	one+table+dish a full table of dishes	152/171/008
桌 + 子 桌子	table+surffix table	171/172
饭 + 桌 饭桌	meal+table dining table	026/171
几桌	several tables	052/171
这桌	this table	167/171
那桌	that table	85/171
小桌	small table	143/171
桌椅	tables and chairs	171/155

Example Sentences

1/171	Chinese	我有一个很大的书桌。
	English	I have a big desk.
2/171	Chinese	妈妈做了一桌菜。
	English	Mother made a full table of dishes.
3/171	Chinese	这里有几桌菜?
	English	How many tables of dishes are there?
4/171	Chinese	爸爸上个星期六去商店买了一些桌椅。
	English	Dad went to the store and bought some tables and chairs last Saturday.
5/171	Chinese	谢老师的爸爸是东北人，今天这桌东北菜都是他爸爸做的。
	English	Teacher Xie's father comes from the Northeast. Today all the dishes on this table featuring the culinary tradition of his hometown were cooked by him.

子 child/son/person zǐ; suffix zi 172 | Z

Chinese	English	Character codes
车 + 子 车子	vehicle+suffix vehicle	010/172
本 + 子 本子	notebook+suffix notebook	006/172
杯 + 子 杯子	cup+suffix cup; glass	004/172
儿子	son+suffix son	024/172
点子	point+suffix idea	016/172
个子	height	031/172
影子	shadow	156/172
椅子	chair	155/172
样子	look+suffix appearance	151/172
子女	son+female children	172/091

Example Sentences

1/172	Chinese	这本本子是米老师买的。
	English	The notebook is bought by Teacher Mi.
2/172	Chinese	我喜欢你高兴时候的样子。
	English	I like how you look when you are happy.
3/172	Chinese	他没有子女。
	English	He has no children.
4/172	Chinese	这个很好看的杯子是妈妈的。
	English	This good-looking cup belongs to my mother.
5/172	Chinese	高老师有很多点子，汉语课的学生们都很喜欢他。
	English	All the students like Teacher Gao's Chinese lessons as he has a lot of ideas.

Z | 173　字 character zì

Chinese	English	Character codes
打 + 字 打字	knock+character type	013/173
很 + 多 + 字 很多字	very+many+character a lot of words	043/023/173
大 + 字 大字	big+character big character; calligraphy	014/173
小字	small+character small print	143/173
写字	write characters	146/173
汉字	Chinese character	038/173

Example Sentences

1/173	Chinese	今天老师听写了十个汉字。
	English	Today the teacher dictated ten Chinese characters.
2/173	Chinese	汉字是不是不好学?
	English	Are Chinese characters difficult to learn or not?
3/173	Chinese	你喜欢写字还是打字?
	English	Do you like writing or typing?
4/173	Chinese	我和姐姐不一样，她喜欢写汉字，我不那么喜欢。
	English	My elder sister and I are not the same. She likes to write Chinese characters, but I don't quite like it.
5/173	Chinese	我写的大字很不好看。老师说，大字不好写，天天写会好一些。
	English	The calligraphy I wrote was not pretty at all. My teacher said, 'Writing calligraphy is not easy. If you practise every day, you will improve.'

租 rent/lease zū 174 | Z

Chinese	English	Character codes
租 + 车 租车	rent + vehicle car rental	174/010
租车 + 店 租车店	car rental shop	174/010/018
出 + 租 出租	out + rent rent	012/174
打出租车	take + taxi take a taxi	013/012/174/010
租衣服	rent clothes	174/153/029
月租	monthly rent	162/174
年租	annual rent	090/174

Example Sentences

1/174	Chinese	我坐出租车去饭店。	
	English	I will take a taxi to the hotel.	
2/174	Chinese	在中国，你会打出租车吗?	
	English	Do you know how to call a taxi in China?	
3/174	Chinese	我租了很多漂亮的衣服。	
	English	I rented a lot of nice clothes.	
4/174	Chinese	这个书店的月租是多少钱?	
	English	What is the monthly rent for this bookshop?	
5/174	Chinese	我妈妈明年想出租她的菜店，去租一个饭馆儿。	
	English	Next year, my mother wants to lease out her grocery store and then open a restaurant.	

Z | 175　昨 yesterday zuó

Chinese	English	Character codes
昨 + 天 昨天	yesterday	175/128
昨天 + 上午 昨天上午	yesterday morning	175/128/108/134
昨天下午	yesterday afternoon	175/128/139/134

Example Sentences

1/175	Chinese	昨天下雨了。
	English	It rained yesterday.
2/175	Chinese	爸爸昨天上午去医院了。
	English	Dad went to the hospital yesterday morning.
3/175	Chinese	昨天的雨很大。
	English	The rain was heavy yesterday.
4/175	Chinese	学校昨天开学，我看见了很多老师和同学，大家都很高兴。
	English	Yesterday was the first day of the new term. I met a lot of teachers and students. All of us were very happy.
5/175	Chinese	米老师的爸爸昨天住院了，住的是工人医院。
	English	Teacher Mi's father was hospitalized yesterday afternoon in the Worker's Hospital.

作 do / done / write / compose / work zuò 176 | Z

Chinese	English	Character codes
作 + 家 作家	writer	176/053
写 + 作 写作	write+compose writing	146/176
习 + 作 习作	practice+compose composition exercise	136/176
工作	labour+work work; job	032/176
做工作	do+work do a job	178/032/176

Example Sentences

1/176	Chinese	我想做一个作家。	
	English	I want to become a writer.	
2/176	Chinese	小明的爸爸妈妈都是作家。	
	English	Little Ming's mum and dad are both writers.	
3/176	Chinese	你爱写作吗?	
	English	Do you love writing?	
4/176	Chinese	这是我上个星期的习作，你喜欢吗?	
	English	This was my composition exercise last week. Do you like it?	
5/176	Chinese	我去年在西北认识了一个中国的作家，听说他很有名气。	
	English	Last year I met a Chinese writer in the Northwest. I heard that he is famous.	

Z | 177　坐 sit/travel by zuò

Chinese	English	Character codes
坐 + 车 坐车	sit+car take a car	177/010
不 + 坐 不坐	do not sit	007/177
坐 + 下 坐下	sit down	177/139
坐飞机	sit+fly+machine take a plane	177/027/051
坐火车	sit+fire+vehicle take a train	177/050/010
坐出租车	take a taxi	177/012/174/010

Example Sentences

1/177	Chinese	飞机和火车你喜欢坐哪个?
	English	Given plane and train, which do you prefer to travel by?
2/177	Chinese	高小姐喜欢坐在那个椅子上看书。
	English	Miss Gao likes to sit on that chair and read books.
3/177	Chinese	你是什么时候坐的飞机?
	English	When did you take the plane?
4/177	Chinese	爸爸明天坐出租车去饭店。
	English	Dad will take a taxi to the hotel tomorrow.
5/177	Chinese	我不坐爸爸的车去北京，我开车去。
	English	I will not take my father's car to Beijing. I'll drive there.

做 make / do / produce zuò 178 | Z

Chinese	English	Character codes
不 + 做 不做	not do	007/178
做 + 菜 做菜	cook dishes	178/008
做 + 衣 + 服 做衣服	make clothes	178/153/029
做对	do+right do correctly	178/022
做饭	make+food cooking	178/026
好做	good+do easy to do	39/178
想做	want+do want to do	142/178

Example Sentences

1/178	Chinese	我不会做中国菜，你会不会?	
	English	I don't know how to cook Chinese food. Do you know how to cook?	
2/178	Chinese	我们小学的谢老师做的菜很好吃。	
	English	The dishes Teacher Xie of our primary school cooks are delicious.	
3/178	Chinese	今天是星期天，你想做什么?	
	English	Today is Sunday. What do you want to do?	
4/178	Chinese	谢老师说他的儿子什么都不想做，他很生气。	
	English	Teacher Xie says his son doesn't like to do anything. He is very angry about it.	
5/178	Chinese	我在大学学的是医学，我很想做一个好医生。	
	English	I studied medicine at university. I want to be a good doctor.	

附录

范氏序法 *

"序法——汉语之法则"最理想的使用者，通常是那些没有教过中文，或对一般文法的主谓宾、定状补没有概念的人。言外之意是，如果你是一位有经验的对外汉语的老师，那么就请尽量忘记固有的文法概念，给"序法"腾出位子，让它进入你的脑子。

一、序法

先说"序法"。我们不谈这个法则的抽象概念，而从形象入手。

我们可以把"序法"视作一部摄影机，开机后便不停地拍摄，拍摄后也不做任何剪接与编辑，仅做实拍纪录。那么，情形会怎么样呢？

摄影计划：

锁定角色1：太阳（选择一个全天有阳光的日子）
纪录时间：日出到日落
纪实情况：1. 太阳在东边的地平线处发出青光；2. 露出一点；3. 渐渐升起；4. 脱离地平线；5. 向中天运行；6. 在中天；7. 向西边前行；8. 接近西边的地平线；9. 部分沉入西边的地平线；10. 从西边消失。

锁定角色2：岩浆
纪录时间：数万年
纪实情况：1. 岩浆在地球深处聚集；2. 向四处流动；3. 找到了山峰的突破处；4. 积聚能量；5. 冲出山峰形成火山口；6. 喷向天空；7. 流向大地或海洋；8. 失去能量渐渐冷却；9. 形成土地或岛屿。

锁定角色3：你（或任何动物）
纪录时间：一天24小时
纪实情况：1. 你在睡觉；2. 早上起床；3. 吃早点；4. 离开家；5. 开车去上班；6. 在班上工作；7. 吃午餐；8. 做下午工作；9. 开车回家；10. 吃晚饭；11. 看书（看电视）；12. 上床睡觉；13. 睡到第二天早上。

锁定角色4：麦子
纪录时间：数个月
纪实情况：1. 麦种埋进耕地；2. 出苗；3. 成长；4. 出穗；5. 成熟。

---

* 之所以名范氏，原因有二。一者，作者苏立群先生出身苏州范家，系范蠡及范仲淹的延世子孙，苏姓是家族北迁后作为艺术活动的"艺姓"。序法以范姓冠名，体现归真与承传之意。再者，序法亦是钩沉，用"范"既有无意独揽，又有归纳、规范之意。

如果这部摄影机以每一个镜头捕捉到的景象来"定一个胶片的画格"和配上对应的文字的话，那么"太阳"就有 10 个画格，有 10 段文字。这 10 段文字连在一起，就是十句很好的中文；"岩浆"有 9 个格，也是 9 段很好的中文；"你"有 13 个格，即有 13 段很好的中文；"麦子"有 5 个格，情况也是一样。简言之，摄影机拍下胶片的格序就是汉语表达意思的序法——顺序、次序之法。更重要的是这些画格、也就是汉语的字词都具有"不可调换位置"（简称"不可调位"）的特性。

诚然，以上是人类观察世界的角度。如果从大宇宙的角度（也可称之为"天眼"）来看，应该得出这样的结论：**序法就是自然法则。即，万物以何种形式发生，这个形式以何种方式运动，其运动的结果又是什么，这一切都是自然而然的。而把这个次序用文字纪录下来，就是汉语语序的实质所在。**

现在再来看看具体的，细小的方面。

举一个长长的、标准的陈述句为例：

我明天早上得去飞机场把一个从英国伦敦来的、只在北京开一天会的代表团送到市中心的希尔顿酒店。

全句 43 个字。这 1-43 的顺序就是 43 个电影胶片的画格，一格接一格，其顺序如同那四个"锁定的角色"一样，具有"不可调位"性。其中明天、早上、飞机场、英国、伦敦、北京、代表团、城中心、希尔顿、酒店，是由 10 个单个汉字构造起来的词，意味深长的是这 10 个词也呈现了"不可调位"的"字序"（序法的元素形式）。比如"明天"，"明"在这里是时间的字词，"天"是长度的字词，组构在一起，就形成了"明天"的词义。"早上"也是同样，"早"是时间的字词，"上"是时间段的字词，组构在一起就表达了"早上"的词义。以此类推，10 个词都是一样的组构顺序。包括"飞机场"，3 个单独的字串构在一起："飞"是运动的方式，"机"是此物具有的机械属性，"飞机"是"飞行的机械"，"飞"修饰、限定（下文简称"修限"）了"机"，如果把修限词"飞"换成"手"，就是"手机"。如果把"机"这个被修限的字换成"鸟"，就成了"飞鸟"。顺着这个思路，"飞机 – 场"，也是"飞机"修限"场"。如果把"场"换成"库"，"飞机库"就变成另一个词义了。以上这些，表明了由一个**"单个汉字"**构成两个或两个以上的词的**"字序规律"。**

下一步的解析是，10 个"组构的词"与其他 20 个"单字词"，是以何种规则连在一起来生成句义的。我们再把"天眼"牌的摄影机架上，可以看到它拍下来的画格顺序正是"我 – 明天 – 早上 – 得 – 去 – 飞机场 – 把 – 一 – 个 – 从 – 英国 – 伦敦 – 来 – 的、只 – 在 – 北京 – 开 – 一 – 天 – 会 – 的 – 代表团 – 送 – 到 – 市中心 – 的 – 希尔顿 – 酒店。"这个 1-43 的顺序，与话语者用一个陈述句告诉我们他明天早上要做的事情的先后顺序完全一致。更进一层，**不论这句话是发生在未来（我们的例子）、平时还是过去，其顺序都不会改变：**

请看平时（只改一个字，但其字位不变）：

我（明）每天早上得去飞机场把一个从英国伦敦来的、只在北京开一天会的代表团送到市中心的希尔顿酒店。

过去（改一个字，但其字位不变；加两个"了"表示行为动作的完成）：

我昨天早上（得）去了飞机场把一个从英国伦敦来的、只在北京开一天会的代表团送到了市中心的希尔顿酒店。

……回到语言学的层面，我们用两句话便可以概括"序法"的规律：**汉语的语法是"我口说我做，我手记我为。"**

这个陈述句的语序可以说得更清楚，更具体化：

a."我"与"明天"不可以调位，因为这个话语者是从今天（或当下）在说未来的"明天"所要做的事，所以"我"的字词位一定要在"明天"字词位的前边。

b."明天"与"早上"不可调位，因为先有"明天"然后才有"早上"。

c."去飞机场"不可与"明天早上"调位，因为话语者出发去飞机场的时间是明天的早上，时间在前，行为动作在后，调位则违反实际生活的顺序。

d."一个从英国伦敦来的""只在北京开一天会的"，这两个短句都是在修限后面的"代表团"，说明此团的特点，不可倒置。

e."送到－市中心的－希尔顿－酒店。"这个四词素也不可调位，因为"送"必须有一个地点可去，"到"是到达。"送到"组构是：先"送"，才能"到"。送到什么地方呢？希尔顿的酒店在北京有几个，而字词的排列顺序告诉我们，要先去"市中心"，尔后才能抵达"希尔顿"。希尔顿什么？不是饭馆或其他的处所，是"酒店"，因此，"希尔顿""置于"酒店"的前面，也不可调位。

因此，如果把这个长句换作我们以上列出的第三个锁定角色"你"，那么你要陈述你明天的计划，完全就是"天眼所纪录"的顺序，无一例外。总括起来说，**汉语没有语法，有的仅是如实地记录万物发生、发展的过程，是"自然之法"，即"序法"。**

二、 词性

再以那个长句做例：

我明天早上得去飞机场把一个从英国伦敦来的、只在北京开一天会的代表团送到市中心的希尔顿酒店。

43个字里，有40个汉字，或者说，19个单独字和10个组构词，都有它们各自的字义和词义，但是有一个出现了三次的字"的"，没有字义。更实际的说法是，这个"的"字无法翻译成其他的文字——这类的特殊的字在"序法"里称作"虚词"。**虚词在现代汉语里为数不多，据统计，虚词仅占全部字词的4%左右。除了这很小的份额，其他的字词在"序法"里统称为"实词"。这里试着下一个定论："汉语是由实词与虚词串连在一起构成的语言。"**

虚词，顾名思义，就是不实之词，没有固定的词义（即无法译成其他的语言），也没有衍生与组构其他词的功能。虚词在汉语句子中的功用是"言简意赅"。从审美来说，虚词的嵌入能使句子更具有美感、乐感。以语言学而论，是汉语的"语法码"，以"序法"而言，是序法码。

这些序法码具有三个特点（再以那个长长的陈述句为例）：

1. 它们能将相同或不同的词性或短语连接起来。如，"只在北京开一天会**的**代表团"（"**的**"出现在短语"北京开一天会"的后面，以修限位于"**的**"后面的"代表团"——说明是一个什么样的团）。

2. 它们服从"序法"的总规则，具有按部就班、不可调位的特性："从英国伦敦来的、只在北京开一天会的代表团送到市中心的希尔顿酒店。"三个**"的"**的字位都非常恰当，不能放在其他的位置。

3. 虚词有**"可被删除"**性。即，一篇文章如果把占 4% 的虚词摘除，其内容依然可以表述。如"我明天早上得去飞机场把一个从英国伦敦来（的）、只在北京开一天会（的）代表团送到市中心（的）希尔顿酒店。"删去虚词，人们照样看得懂也听得懂，只是不舒服而已。

其实，"序法"的规律在中国南北朝时期就由刘勰（465—521）在他的名著《文心雕龙》里提出过，他说："置言有位……，位言曰句"，即，**说话放置字词要有顺序，有了字词顺序后才能产生句义。**用现代的话说就是**"汉语是一种字词有固定位置的语言"**。

既然字词如此重要，了解它们的分类就十分必要了。

第一类：实词

实词是那些"有固定词义，并且具有衍生与组构功能的字词"。据统计，汉语中实词的使用占文章全部字词的 96% 左右。

实词有以下六类：	
1. 名词	我，他们，北京，图书馆，五十，杯……
2. 动词	1) 普通动词：吃，喝，走，打，想，觉得，……
	2) 系词（维系两端，表示关系）：是，在，有，当，等于，大于，红于……
3. 形容词	也称感判词，与英语不同，汉语的此类词皆具有动词的功能：冷，大，舒服，红，热闹……
4. 度词	1) 时间度词：
	a. 频度：常常，也，不常，经常，反复，总（是），老是，无时无刻……
	b. 速度：快，慢慢，刻不容缓，急切……
	c. 规则度：得，必须，应该，愿意，打算……
	2) 空间度词：
	a. 程度：很，非常，无与伦比……
	b. 尺度：只，仅仅……
	c. 幅度：大多，一五一十……
5. 介词	1) 对等介词：和，与，同，跟……
	2) 非对等介词：为，比，替，对，向，往……
	3) 固定搭配介词：因为……所以……；虽然……但是……；又……又……；既……也……，在……上/下/里/外/方面……
6. 疑问词	谁，什么，哪儿，为什么，怎么，怎么样……

第二类：虚词——序法码

常用虚词分类：虚词——的、地、得、过、着、了。

1. 修饰限定虚词

的	我＋的＋书	图书馆＋的＋书	有用＋的＋书	买＋的＋书
	人称代名词＋的＋名词	名词＋的＋名词	形容词＋的＋名词	动词＋的＋名词
	以代名词去修限名词	以名词去修限名词	以形容词去修限名词	以动词去修限名词
地	同情＋地＋说	不知所云＋地＋说		
	形容词＋地＋动词	形容语＋地＋动词		
	形容词修限动词	成语/习语/短语修限动词		
得	好＋得＋无法形容	流利＋得＋像中国人一样		
	形容词＋得＋度词	形容词＋得＋短语		
	形容词修饰限定度词	形容词修饰限定短语		
过	去＋过＋北京	当＋过＋老师		
	动词＋过＋名词	动词＋过＋名词		
	动词修饰限定名词，突出名词意义	动词修饰限定名词		
着	看＋着＋书	热＋着＋呢	站＋着＋看＋书	
	动词＋着＋名词	形容词＋着＋虚词	动词＋着＋动词＋名词	
	动词修限名词	形容词修限虚词	动词修饰动词、名词	

2. 完成/改变虚词 "了"

了	去＋了＋北京	去＋北京＋了	是＋老师＋了
	动词＋了＋名词	动词、名词＋了	动词＋名词＋了
	动作不继续	事件已完成	名语后面＋了，表示以前不曾有/不曾是，而现在有/是了。

3. 疑问虚词： 吗、吧、呢。

4. 象声虚词： 呼呼、哗啦……

5. 感叹虚词： 呀、啊……

三、特殊动词"把""被"和"是……的"句型

"把"的第三声是动词，通常用在"把门""把住"。**"把字句"是一个话语者希求通过行为改变现状以达新状态的句型**（这个句式一定会有两个或两个以上的动词），如果用汉语直白地替换这个动词"把"，其短句就是——"握住XX，且使其改变成什么样"的句式。比如："**请把门打开！**"其实是在说："**请握住门而且使其打开！**"

为什么绕这么大的弯子解释这个"把"字句呢？原因很简单，因为在印欧语系里没有与汉语"把"字结构对等字词和句式。再者，"把"字如果不是常用字还好，可它却是一个高频字！为此，欧美那些有中文系的大学，无一例外地把解释"把"这个中文句式作为特殊的语言现象而列为高学位的研究课题，即博士学位。实际上，按照序法，这个句型无非就是一个"**双动以达希求结果**"的句子而已，"**请把门打开！**""**把**"（**握住**）是第一动，"**打开**"是第二动。**话语者的希求是改变门关着的状态而要求打开。**

不像"把"字句，"被"字句在英语里是使用频繁的句型；不过英语使用时更客观，可以说，英语以"天眼"来描述被动语态。如"花被水浇了""墙被工人粉刷了""信被邮递员送来了"等这些如实地描绘，同时英语也有如同汉语的"手机被偷了""房子被水淹了"这一类非本愿的、由外力强制发生的用法。究其原因是，**汉语把"被字句"与社会的分工结合了起来**，认为"工人粉刷墙"是他们的工作所决定的，同样"邮递员送信"也是社会分工，所以不必强调这个事实的客观性。

再一个特别的句型为"**是……的**"句。比如"我妈妈是昨天来北京的"。其实，这个句子是"古语今用，推陈出新"。用文言文的说法是"吾娘者，乃昨日至北京者也！"再如"这个人是不吃肉的"。即"其人者，乃不食肉者也！"看了后就知道，这两句话都是"是"字句："我妈妈是昨天来北京的（妈妈）"，"这个人是不吃肉的（人）"，出于语言"自性"的省略功能，于是就把句子结束在"的"上。从音律学来讲，倒是"此处无声胜有声"，成为一种强调的句型。列一个公式：

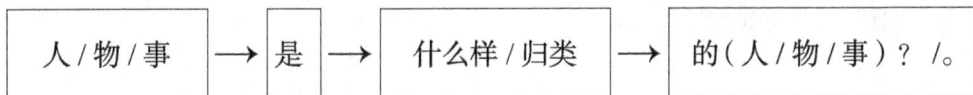

| 人/物/事 | → | 是 | → | 什么样/归类 | → | 的（人/物/事）？/。 |

再回到以上的举两个"人"的例句为：

人/物/事	是	什么样/**归类**	的（**人**/物/事——省略）
我妈妈	是	昨天来北京	的（归那类/拨人中的一个）。
这个人	是	不吃肉	的（那类人中的一个）。

再列举两个"物"的例子：

人 / **物** / 事	是	什么样 / **归类**	的（人 / **物** / 事——省略）
你这个手机	是	在哪儿买	的（归类于地区——手机被省略）？
这个房子	是	用银行贷款买	的（归类于钱获得的方式——房子被省略）。

再列举两个"事"的例子：

人 / 物 / **事**	是	什么样 / **归类**	的（人 / 物 / **事**——省略）
这件事	是	不可以说	的（归类于隐私——事被省略）。
这个规定	是	很严格	的（归类于条款——规定被省略）。

　　我们从汉语句子的结构方面讲了序法，又从组成句子的字词方面讲了实词、虚词两大类，还将汉语动词中两个特殊的句式"把""被"以及"是……的"以归类方式的强调句做了大致的介绍。下一步就是如何把以上的概念运用到具体的教学之中，消除那些初学汉语的人对一门非印欧语系语言的恐惧。我们的做法是以**五个母句**作为开门见山的第一章。

四、五个母句

　　这个来自序法的"五他"，即，他是谁？他做什么？他有什么？他在哪儿？他怎么样？这是人类在远古荒蛮时代天天都要面对的问题。那个时候，有了表达"五他"的语言方式，就可以达到沟通的目的。后来随着人类社会的发展和进步，语言越来越丰富，但是万变不离其宗，都是从这五个方面衍化出来的。请注意，在序法里，我们把"是""有""在"都归于系动词。

请看下表。

	陈述句		此类动词	例句 / 注释
句型1	他是老师。 他不是老师。 他是教汉语的（归类省略了人）。		姓 / 叫 / 当 大于 / 小于 / 等于……	他姓王。 他当老师。 他的收入高于别人。 血浓于水。 北京大于天津。 他不等于我。
	结构：名词＋是系词＋名词			
	类型： 左右对等句（是 / 姓…） 左右 / 非等句（大于…）			

续表

	陈述句	此类动词	例句/注释
句型2	他教汉语。 他不教汉语。 结构：名词+动词+名词 类型：**动作行为句**	此类动词数量巨大：吃/喝/看/睡/做/写/打/跑/想/等/演/出版/觉得/……	特别句型：形动词/自动词
			1.形动（形容词也是动词）：他胖了/他出名了/他难过了/他冷了/他犹豫了。
			结构：名词+形动+了
			2.自动（主体自身动词）：他哭了/他来了/他病了。
			结构：名词+自身动词+了
句型3	他有汉语书。 结构：名词+有系词+名词 类型：**归属句**	（拥）有……	注意：其句式的否定式是"没"： 他没有汉语书。
句型4	他在教室。 结构：名词+在系词+名词 类型：**空间地点句** 他在看书。 结构：名词+在系词+动词+名词 类型：**时间行为句**	在、于（多用于文言文）	注意：其否定式的"不"与"没"都可以使用，但产生的句义不同。
句型5	他（很）认真。 结构：名词+形容词 类型：**形容判断句**	好/坏/努力/用功/聪明/高/壮/伶俐/清楚/明了/深刻/……	注意：这个句型包括比较句——他比我认真。

	句型2的变形句		注释
把字句	**把字句用于"通过行动改变事物的现状"。** 请大家把书打开！ 请你把那本书给我。 **动词"把"**+名词+动词+改变后的新状态		句式2的双动词句
被字句	**被字句用于"事物的改变迫于外力所强加"。** 教室的窗子**被**（那个学生）打破了。 名词+**动词"被"**+（外力名词）+动词+了		句式2的双动词句

这五个基本句是从千千万万个汉语句子中提炼出来的，具有代表性。任何一句话，都来自五个句子中的一种或是它们之间的排列组合。

如，"他在中学教英语。"分解后是句式 4+2——他在中学 / 他教英语。

再如，"他在中学教英语比在小学合适。"分解后是句式 4+2+5——他在中学 / 他教英语 / 中学教英语比在小学合适。

再复杂一点，"他在中学教英语有比在小学教英语更多的经验。"分解后是句式 4+2+3+5——他在中学 / 他教英语 / 他有经验 / 中学比小学更多。凡此种种不一一列举。

五、组词与组字构义的小贴士

汉字组词孰先孰后的次序是有一定之规的。这个规矩首先基于"**自然而然**"（时空维度）的次序，犹如老子之说："人法地，地法天，天法道，道法自然。"其次是社会既定的价值观。有《易经 序卦》的一句话为证："有天地然后有万物，有万物然后有男女，有男女然后有夫妇，有夫妇然后有父子，有父子然后有君臣，有君臣然后有上下，有上下然后礼义有所错。"

因此组词分两大类：

第一类：两个平行的、同类的字词组合的顺序

1. 自然而然类——根据物体在宇宙及自然中所占有的时空之先后与大小度排列：

天地，古今，大小，前后，上下，阴阳，远近，老少，父子……

2. 价值观类——随着人类社会的发展及价值观的形成排列的，如：

君臣，男女，夫妻，国家，民族，龙凤，红绿，虎狼，牛马……

第二类：前字词划定大范围，以修限细化后字词

1. 明显的修限

政府，政策，政治，政纲，政党，政务……"政"是大范畴。

飞机，飞船，飞碟，飞弹，飞行，飞鸟……"飞"是大范畴。

湖水，湖泊，湖蓝，湖蟹，湖怪，湖色……"湖"是大范畴。

乐天，乐趣，乐土，乐园，乐意，乐得……"乐"是大范畴。

2. 潜在的修限

漂亮："漂"洗干净后才能鲜"亮"。舒服："舒"展后才能"服"帖。美丽：审"美"在先而后靓"丽"。得意：先获"得"后方能满"意"。庄严："庄"重在先，"严"肃才能体现……

3. 动词直接修限动词 / 形容词

跑 – 完，做 – 好，关 – 上，写 – 出，说 – 清楚，抓 – 紧……

4. 动词通过虚词（得）间接修限动词 / 形容词：

跑 – 得 – 完，做 – 得 – 好，关 – 得 – 上，写 – 得 – 对，说 – 得 – 清楚，抓 – 得 – 紧……

5. 形容词通过虚词（地）间接修限动词：

很快－地－跑完，清楚－地－说明，准确－地－写出，刻不容缓－地－抓紧，严严实实－地－关上……

6. 成语的序法装配：

守－株－待－兔，刻－舟－求－剑，唇－亡－齿－寒，口－蜜－腹－剑，得－陇－望－蜀，狐－假－虎－威，得－寸－进－尺，龙－飞－凤－舞，狼－狈－为－奸，亦－步－亦－趋……

以上成语都显示出字位的"不可调位"特性，不然这些故事会变成另一番样子。

六、总论

首先，汉语是"序法"语言，**其句义是由字词排列的前后顺序来决定的。**汉语序法体现在一句话中，一定是前字限定、修饰后字；前词限修后词；前句（包括分句）限修后句；直至句末（序尾）"核心目的词"（以下简称"核目词"）的出现，句义才呈现。因而，从总的行文规律方面体现了其"趋真向实"的渐进性。**换言之，汉语句子在行文没有完成、核目词没有出现时，无法判断句义。或，句义是由字词从头至尾逐渐积累起来的时空信息最后总地交给句末的核目词来决定。**比如我们反复做例的"我明天早上得去飞机场把一个从英国伦敦来的、只在北京开一天会的代表团送到市中心的希尔顿酒店。"全句数十个字词，直到"希尔顿酒店"这个"核目词"出现，才形成句义。如果这个核目词是"去参观"，那么句义就迥异了。因此，在核目词的前面，无论字词有多少，都是在一步一步地积累信息，最后由核目词"希尔顿酒店"或"去参观"来决定句义。

其次是汉语的句式。在序法的总则下，汉语句式分三类：

陈述句式。此类属自然顺序类，即词序为：1.时间（天为）；2.地点（地为）；3.行为（人为）。"我明天早上得去飞机场把一个从英国伦敦来的、只在北京开一天会的代表团送到市中心的希尔顿酒店。""明天早上"是时间，"飞机场"是地点，其后的部分是行动。这一句式占正式文体、包括口头表达的绝大多数。而这个"无语法结构，仅复制自然顺序"的特点，是全人类的生存习性，已超越了语言学、社会学的范畴。

语气／语境句式。除了句末的核目词以外，其他词可随语气或语境的需要进行调整；但是，核目词始终处于句末的规律不变。这一句式主要用于日常会话和艺术语言。

韵律句式。以文言文与诗词格律为多，句末时为核目词，时为韵律所需之词。

范氏序法千字文

子　汉文语言以序为本，字植于序，循"负阴而抱阳""文以载道"之则。

"字"乃最小之单位，"序"乃串字之法则。凡字含本义与衍义者归"实字"，仅表语法之义者为"虚字"。

"序"乃"道序"、自然之序。以字为素，序"字"而生词，序"字、词"而生句，序"句"而生段，序"段"而生章。

丑　人乃物灵之首，语言之丰非他物可比。

"人"知万物本无名，无名则难分，于是上者名"天"，下者名"地"，万物亦逐一得名，物灵之首则自谓之"人"。遂"是"字始创，"是"句乃生。

人见万物之存各有其位：天在上，地在下，万物居中。于是言位之字"在"乃生，言存之字"有"始行。

人识万物各有其质，而质各有其征：天之"阔"征也，地之"实"征也，日之"耀"征也，月之"清"征也，山之"巍"、水之"滢"征也。言万物之征谓之诉性。于是"判性"之句滋生。

人困于世，饮、食、男、女皆动之所获；动则生，无动则殆。"饮""食""男""女"诸动无日可离。于是"动"字句乃生。

综上所述，后世千言，皆源"是""有""在""动""判"人生五要之需、之合、之展。

寅　汉文之行止，先天后地再人。

一句伊始，先表"何时""何地"后而"何为"。"文道"遵天道、自然之道。无天地之托依，人何存？文何有？

古占卜，天时、地利、人为；传至后世，遂成文则。概之，一言既出，天、地之需先于人，人先于动，动先于果。无天、地、人、动，则无果。盖凡言，依天地人动果之序。

卯　汉文句式。

汉文句式分三：一叙事，其序天地人动果；二言情，以情至为果，重词则后置。"去看电影院，你们都？"重词为"都"；三咏诗作赋，以辞美为果，美韵垫后。

辰　汉字库甚巨，然仅分两支，一为实，二为虚。

实者具内涵可延、外构有力之功能；**虚字**乃文法码，仅限定修饰、言简意赅之用。实、虚两支相辅相成，以天—地—人—动—果之序行文。

实字存五类：物称为**名**（包括数与量），物行为**动**，物征为**判**，评判为**度**，物串为**连**或**介**。虽五，无固，判可动，动可名，动判相构则文法出：动动；动判；判动；判判是也。

虚者文法码也：**的**，修限，码植名前。**地**，修限，码植判后、动前。**得**，修限，码植动后、判前，判后、度前。**了**，限定或言变，居位有四，于诸动、动名、名或判后。**过**，限定，码植动后，以凸名状。**在动**，以时锁动，动延。**动着**，以空锁动，动滞。"把""被"皆具"虚实双性"：**把**，达愿，甲挚乙动求达甲愿。**被**，迫受，甲迫受乙动之果。**是……的**，以"归类"明态、释惑。**就**，主褒超常（偶贬、述）。**才**，主贬超常（偶褒、述）。**吗**，疑问。**呢**，简略疑问。**吧**，半疑问。

巳　套组。

因为……，**所以**……；**在**……**上**；**以**……**为**……；**用**……**来**……；……套句需知套词之构、之用。

午　成语（习语）。

成语（习语）多四言，行文循或趋真或趋美之规，组构式达九类之多，不赘。

跋：
酝酿数年　一朝面世

自从我提出"'序法'是汉文语法"的理论，到如今能出版这套教材，前前后后经历了二十个年头。

二十年来，我一直用这段话给自己和我们的老师们鼓气："不要羁绊于西方语言学家对我们语言下的定义；作为中国人，对汉语'自性'的研究是我们义不容辞的责任。"

正源于此，我要诚心诚意地感谢外文局麾下的华语教学出版社，感谢他们的见识与勇气；也要感谢成立于 2006 年的英国子午文院（Meridian Chinese Studies）对"序法"理论的研究、开发以及长达 14 年的课堂实践，正是这些因素使得这套教材日趋成熟。

这里给"序法"冠以"范氏"做一个注脚：我是苏州范家的子孙，苏姓是家父北迁后作为艺术活动的"艺姓"。我家祖上有范蠡、范仲淹，序法这一点点小成就当属祖宗的福荫，为此称之为"范氏序法"。再，百多年前，清人马建忠首次以印欧语系解构汉文，著《马氏文通》，汉文在马氏西语"他性"的解释下流行至今。"范氏序法"力求返璞归真，重新回到汉文本身，尝试以其"自性"诠释语法规律。

整套书并非学术大著，又是针对外国学生，所以亦庄亦谐，以学习效果为主，学术依据为辅。每次碰到需用古字（甲骨文和篆体）的字符解构简化字体时，我都尽量寻找源头，但牵强乃至穿凿附会依然在所难免，还请读者和老师们谅解。

作者、主编　苏立群
2020.10 于英国伦敦

出版策划：王君校　韩　晖
统筹协调：付　眉　韩　颖　彭　博
策划编辑：陆　瑜
责任编辑：陆　瑜
英文编辑：韩芙芸

图书在版编目（CIP）数据

60小时突破初级中文．课本．上册：汉英／苏立群主编．-- 北京：华语教学出版社，2021.4
　ISBN 978-7-5138-2063-9

Ⅰ．①6⋯　Ⅱ．①苏⋯　Ⅲ．①汉语－对外汉语教学－教材　Ⅳ．①H195.4

中国版本图书馆CIP数据核字（2020）第264880号

60小时突破初级中文．课本（上册）

LIQUN SU（苏立群）　主编

*

©华语教学出版社有限责任公司
华语教学出版社有限责任公司出版
（中国北京百万庄大街24号　邮政编码 100037）
电话：(86)10-68320585　68997826
传真：(86)10-68997826　68326333
网址：www.sinolingua.com.cn
电子信箱：hyjx@sinolingua.com.cn
北京虎彩文化传播有限公司印刷
2021年（16开）第1版
2021年第1版第1次印刷
ISBN 978-7-5138-2063-9
008000